Walking the Triangulation Points of Sussex

David Bathurst

Photographs by David Bathurst

S. B. Publications

BY THE SAME AUTHOR

The Selsey Tram
Six Of The Best
The Jennings Companion
Financial Penalties
Around Chichester In Old Photographs
Here's A Pretty Mess!
Magisterial Lore
The Beaten Track (republished as The Big Walks Of Great Britain)
Poetic Justice
That's My Girl
Walking The Coastline Of Sussex
Best Sussex Walks
Let's Take It From The Top
Walking The Disused Railways Of Sussex
Once More From The Top
Sussex Top Tens
Walking The Kent Coast From End To End
Walking The South Coast Of England
Walking The Riversides Of Sussex
Anyone For Tenors?

To Chester

First published in 2009 by S.B. Publications
14 Bishopstone Road, Seaford, East Sussex
Tel: 01323 893498   Email: sbpublications@tiscali.co.uk

© David Bathurst (Text) 2008
© David Bathurst (Photographs) 2008

ISBN 978-185770-3450

Designed and Typeset by EH Graphics, East Sussex (01273) 515527

CONTENTS

Front Cover: *The Tarring Neville trig point, with the pretty village church just down the hill*

Title Page: *The winter sunshine gives a long shadow to the St Wilfrid's Chapel trig point*

Back Cover: *The Jury's Gap trig point - the most south-easterly in Sussex and the closest trig point to the sea in Sussex*

ABOUT THE AUTHOR

David Bathurst was born in 1959 and has enjoyed writing and walking throughout his adult life. He has walked all the official long-distance footpaths of Great Britain including the South West Coast Path, the Pennine Way and Offa's Dyke Path, and he has also walked the entire south coast of England, his guides to the Sussex and Kent coasts being published by SB Publications in 2002 and 2007 respectively. By profession David is a solicitor and legal adviser to magistrates in Chichester and Worthing. He is married to Susan and has a daughter Jennifer. When not writing or walking he loves vintage sitcom, teashops, and the Times crossword puzzle. His most notable achievements have been the recital of the four Gospels from memory on a single day in 1998 and the recital of the complete works of Gilbert & Sullivan from memory over 4 days in 2007.

AUTHOR'S ACKNOWLEDGEMENTS

I would like to thank Lindsay Woods of SB Publications for her encouragement and support; Mr and Mrs Miller who allowed me to view the trig point situated in their Icklesham back garden; Roger Green of the Littlehampton Gazette whose readers helped me to trace the Brookfield Park, Toddington trig point; Ian Stark and Sue Hanmore of the Lidsey Landfill site who assisted in relation to the trig point previously sited there; my wife Susan for her constant love and forbearance; and my daughter Jennifer who as my frequent walking companion helped to find some of the more elusive trig points that I might otherwise have missed!

INTRODUCTION

One of the most distinctive types of landmark in the British countryside is the triangulation point, or trig point (as I propose, for the sake of convenience, to call them from now on). Many walkers will have passed them, perhaps will be photographed beside one of them, and may have used them as vital navigational aids - without knowing how these extraordinary stone stumps came to decorate the landscape.

Between 1783 and 1853 a task known as the Principal Triangulation was carried out as a means of achieving accurate surveying and mapping of Great Britain. Then, in 1935, the new Director General of the Ordnance Survey(OS), Major-General Malcolm MacLeod, started the retriangulation of Great Britain, an immense task which involved erecting concrete triangulation pillars (trig points) on prominent hilltops throughout England, Wales and Scotland. Every detail of the operation and measurements was carefully specified in advance to endeavour to produce the most accurate measurements possible. Putting up the new trig points frequently required materials and instruments to be carried up hills and mountains on foot. Retriangulation started with a set of several hundred primary trig points, mostly placed on hilltops in order to link with each other across long distances, and then a larger set of around 6000 secondary trig points was added. The operation was not completed till 1962. The results of the retriangulation were subsequently used to create Britain's national grid reference system which would be the basis of the Ordnance Survey's new maps. Achieving a massively improved level of accuracy, retriangulation represented a triumph of the available technology at the time. In recent years, triangulation has been rendered obsolete by satellite-based GPS measurements; as a result, the trig point network is no longer maintained, save for a few trig points that have been re-used by the OS as part of its National GPS network, and sadly some previously existing trig points have now been removed or destroyed. However, the majority have survived and several are now major visitor attractions. About 100 people each month use the TrigpointingUK website to log their visits to trig points, and in the first four years of operation of the site, just over 1100 people have logged at least one visit. Over a dozen people have logged more than 500 trig points each, with the current record standing at 5809 logs. When I contacted the website, this is what I was told by Ian Harris: "Stand on any big peak and watch the walkers as they arrive. Just standing on the summit cairn is not enough for many people; they have to physically touch the trig point. On popular routes, it's not uncommon to see people waiting for their turn to take a group photo by the trig (point), or simply to lay their hands on these monuments, to prove to themselves that they've 'done' the hill. If you include these people in your reckoning, the number of trig point hunters probably numbers in the millions."

The purpose of this book is to provide a definitive guide to discovering all the trig points of Sussex on foot. Sussex boasts more than 130 trig points that are marked on OS maps as such. Some, like those on Chanctonbury Ring, Ditchling Beacon and Firle Beacon, are on hilltops, and provide worthy objectives in the course of an energetic walk. But not all of them are on hilltops. Some are sited rather unceremoniously along the sides of roads or farm tracks. Some are concealed in woodland or in remote and unremarkable countryside where a trig point is the last thing you would expect to find. Many are on private land, and there are even a couple that are in gardens of private houses! There may be many reasons for seeking them out. There is the obvious appeal for the avid collectors who, as mentioned above, wish to log their trig point visits. A good many of them are indeed sited in areas of very great natural beauty, with panoramic views, and the "conquest" of a hilltop trig point will rank as a not inconsiderable achievement. They are significant landmarks and locating them may form the basis of orienteering or "treasure hunt" expeditions. They are a distinctive and interesting part of our heritage and many are worth seeing for their own sake; at least one trig point has been "adopted" and is lovingly maintained by its adoptive owners. And even if you see the trig point as simply a lump of rather unobtrusive concrete, stuck in a thicket or covered in vegetation, it is still an objective and a focus for a brisk walk or a post-pub lunch stroll. You will certainly, in the course of your exploration of them, get to find out a great deal more about the Sussex countryside, including some attractive parts of it that you may not have known even existed. Who knows, once you start, you may wish to build up your own log of trig point visiting and turn it into a significant preoccupation if not obsession. The walks I have described - around 90 in total - vary tremendously in length and difficulty. Some are extremely short, and will work well as a brief pub walk either to gain an appetite for lunch or walk it off afterwards. Some will require a full day or even longer. I have split the book into three discrete sections, one devoted to the trig points of West Sussex, one to the trig points of East Sussex, and a further section is given over to the trig points on the South Downs Way, as I recognise that it may be convenient for those seeking to "bag" the many trig points that lie along its route to walk the trail end-to-end, perhaps (although not necessarily) over a succession of days. All of the walks are accessible by public transport, which is not only more environmentally friendly but provides the possibility of some linear walking, starting and finishing at different locations but with public transport available to get you to the start of and convey you home from the finish of each walk. I have tried, as far as possible, to ensure that the walk has something else of interest to recommend it besides the trig point itself, such as a place of either natural beauty or historic significance, or just a good pub! The preambles to each walk provide all the information you need including OS grid reference for each trig point for that walk, length, degree of difficulty and public transport/refreshment availability although please note the latter detail is subject to constant change. Public transport contact numbers and websites are set out below. Where refreshment provision is limited or non-existent, it is advisable to have supplies of food with you, but ALWAYS carry water and drink it frequently while you walk to prevent thirst. Much of the walking is very easy and no special walking equipment is required for any of the walks. I do recommend a good stout pair of walking shoes or boots, plus appropriate protective clothing in the event of cold, wet or windy weather. You may also like to take the relevant OS map; while the directions given will be sufficient to access and locate each trig point, maps provide a greater detail of the surrounding land which in turn will enhance your enjoyment of the walk. Sketch maps showing the location of the walks are provided, two for West Sussex and two for East Sussex, the numbers on the maps corresponding with the walk number in the text, and also shown are the locations of the starting points of each of the South Downs Way sections (SDW1 denotes location of start of section 1 of the South Downs Way walk, and so on).

So far so good, but there is one problem you will come across time and again in the course of your trig point exploration, which is accessing trig points situated on private land. Many trig points in this book are so situated, and although the law has changed in recent years to allow freer access to parts of the countryside, there is NO general right simply to wander off rights of way if you feel like it. There are many trig points which, although not on public rights of way or access land, can be accessed very easily without obstruction. Others, however, are on land where trespassers certainly are not welcome. The golden rule is - IF UNSURE, SEEK THE OWNER'S PERMISSION. It is acknowledged that this permission may not be easy to obtain, and may involve enquiry of a number of people and/or organisations, but it is the only insurance against being challenged by irate landowners. Trespass itself is not a criminal offence, but intentional damage to property in the course of a trespass certainly is. In some cases discretion will prove the better part of valour, and you may have to be content, as I have had to be on a couple of occasions, to view the trig point from a distance. The relevant text makes it clear whether or not to access a given trig point will require you to enter private land. You may of course choose to take the risk and enter such land without permission, but NEITHER MY PUBLISHER NOR I CAN ACCEPT ANY RESPONSIBILITY FOR THE CONSEQUENCES OF YOUR DOING SO.

BUSES

A number of bus operators provide services referred to in the text. The relevant operator is indicated by initials in the preamble to each walk.

SC - Stagecoach   0845 121 0170
     www.stagecoachbus.com/south

CL - Countryliner   0844 477 1623
     www.countryliner-coaches.co.uk

MB - Metrobus   01293 449191   www.metrobus.co.uk

CB - Compass Bus   01903 690025   www.compass-travel.co.uk

BH - Brighton & Hove   01273 886200   www.buses.co.uk

A - Arriva   0871 200 2233   www.arrivabus.co.uk

ESCC - East Sussex County Council Rider   0871 200 2233   www.eastsussex.gov.uk

CCB - Cuckmere Community Bus   01323 870920
     www.cuckmerebus.freeuk.com

EB - Eastbourne Buses   01323 416416
     www.eastbournebuses.co.uk

(NOTE: at the time of writing it looks likely that Eastbourne Buses will be taken over, possibly by Stagecoach. Please watch for press announcements and check the relevant website.)

Timetables for most routes are posted on the websites shown above.
Please note that sadly many of the bus routes referred to in the text do not operate on Sundays and Bank Holidays. Most of the Stagecoach(SC) routes and all of the Brighton & Hove(BH) routes operate a Sunday and Bank Holiday service, but with the exception of routes between Worthing and Horsham, between Brighton and Horsham via Henfield, Partridge Green and Cowfold, and between Rudgwick and Horsham, and the Cuckmere Community Bus between Berwick and Alfriston, none of the other routes do so at the time of writing. However things do change, sometimes at very short notice, so please check with the relevant operator before travelling.
Whatever your bus travel plans, it may be prudent to have the number of local taxi firms handy, just in case!

TRAINS

Except where stated in the text, all the train services referred to in the text are provided by Southern Trains. All provide a Sunday and Bank Holiday service but often there is weekend engineering work with trains being replaced by buses. For more information ring National Rail Enquiries on 08457 484950.

REFRESHMENTS

The availability of refreshments is shown by the letter R in the preamble to each walk.

P -   pub or pubs

S -   foodstore or stores

C -   café or cafes

Please note that the information provided was correct at the time of writing but changes cannot be ruled out.

West Sussex Walks 1 - 26 and 41
South Downs Way section starts 1 - 3

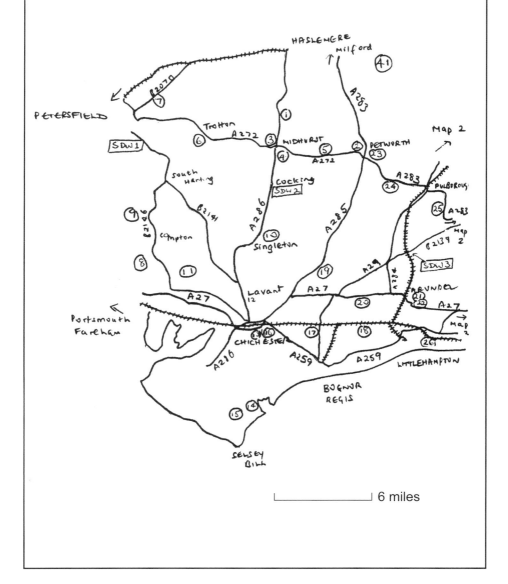

6 miles

~ PART 1 ~
WALKING THE TRIG POINTS OF WEST SUSSEX

1 Verdley/Woolbeding Common SU896253/868264 STRENUOUS.

Regular buses(SC) on Midhurst-Haslemere route stop on A286 at crossroads* with Kings Drive turning for the old King Edward VII Hospital; regular buses(SC) from Midhurst to Chichester, Haslemere and Pulborough. 7 miles. R Henley (P - slightly off route), Midhurst (P,C,S).

Starting from the bus stop asterisked above walk northwards beside the A286 to the brow of the hill, then just as the road begins to descend and swing left, bear right onto a minor road which goes steeply downhill. By continuing along it you'd reach the pretty village of Henley with its very popular pub, but this would be a detour; your route leaves this road shortly after leaving the A286 and as it bends left. Here you bear right onto a signed footpath going very steeply uphill with glorious views to the left (north). As the path levels and a field joins it on the right, take a spur path going very hard right, hairpin-like, and looking south-west from here you can see the Verdley trig point just beyond some old reservoir workings. The trig point itself is not accessible other than by crawling under barbed wire to enter the field, but you can get close enough to it to enjoy good views southwards to the Downs escarpment. Return to the minor road the same

The Verdley trig point on a crisp winter's day

way and retrace your steps to the bus stop at the crossroads asterisked above; turn right into Kings Drive and follow it for just over three quarters of a mile where the road bends and goes forward towards the old hospital entrance. Before the entrance you turn right to continue along the road, soon passing a new housing development which is to your right. The road goes uphill and becomes a rough track; very shortly after it does so there is a footpath signpost** with fingers pointing ahead, left and back the way you've come. Continue along the hilltop track with a NO CARS sign, passing the entrance to Scotland Farmhouse and proceeding through the woods. Follow the track for just over half a mile until it swings sharply right with a PRIVATE sign ahead. On this right bend, you continue along a signed path in the same direction you've been following, then very shortly reach a footpath junction where you turn left, descending steeply under pylons to reach a very narrow road. Cross the road and bear right onto a path that initially goes parallel with the road then swings north-west, giving absolutely glorious views across Woolbeding Common; as the path swings westwards at its highest point, look out for a green path turning to the right and this takes you to the Woolbeding Common trig point. The views across the common are excellent and totally unspoilt. Retrace your steps to the very narrow road and turn right to follow it the short distance to a car park and information board which is to your left. Walk through the car park going straight ahead eastwards to join a path that takes you uphill, back under the

The Woolbeding Common trig point nestling in the bracken

pylons, to a T-junction with a track, turning left to return to the hilltop track, turning right here to follow it back to the signpost double-asterisked above. Turn right here along the bottom end of a car park and very shortly you reach another signed footpath junction; turn left here to follow a delightful footpath downhill through woodland, emerging at a T-junction with a wider track. Turn left then in a few yards reach a fork, taking the left fork here and following the clear path downhill southwards. You reach a crossing track, turning right and then immediately left along a path which arrives at Eastshaw Farm; here the track becomes metalled but the traffic quantity is negligible and it's now a very pleasant walk southwards along this lane to a T-junction with a wider country road. Turn right and follow the road into the pretty village of Woolbeding. Turn left at the T-junction in the village and continue to cross a bridge over the Rother; immediately beyond the bridge turn left onto a signed footpath running eastwards, parallel with the right bank of the river, then striking south-eastwards and rising to the A272 at its junction with June Lane. Bear immediately left into June Lane and follow it all the way into the centre of Midhurst.

2 Stagpark Farm/Peacock's Farm, Northchapel/Black Down
SU961258/965292/919296 STRENUOUS.

Regular buses(SC) serving Petworth on Worthing-Pulborough-Midhurst route; regular buses(SC) serving Haslemere on Guildford-Midhurst route. 12 miles. R Petworth (P,C,S), Colhook(S), Northchapel(P,S), Haslemere(P,C,S).
Note that this is one of the longer walks in this book and may take a full day to complete. Public transport along the route itself is non-existent so if you decide to break the journey at Northchapel (just over halfway) you may want to have some taxi firm numbers handy.

Your walk starts at Petworth's main church, situated on the main A272 on Church Street. Facing outwards from the main church entrance, swing left to follow the A272 along North Street, but very shortly bear left into the Cow Yard entrance to Petworth Park, open daily from 8am until dusk. Observing the footpath direction signs, follow the driveway more or less parallel with the road, past some of the buildings and offices adjacent to Petworth House, then, again as directed, bear left to pass under a tunnel taking you actually underneath part of the Petworth House "complex" and pass through a gate to enter Petworth Park. Walk uphill to a junction of paths, and here bear left to follow a green path that veers gently right, aiming for Upper Pond and keeping the tuftier grass and hillside dotted with trees immediately to the right. On reaching the edge of the pond you bear right along a path, but don't follow the pondside path, rather forking shortly half right along a clear green path uphill; from the top of the rise there

The Stagpark Farm trig point half hidden in hedge

are superb views across Petworth Park and miles of countryside beyond. You then descend steadily through the park, with a profusion of deer on both sides and sometimes on the path itself, although they are remarkably docile and don't seem the least bit fazed by walkers. As you get level with another large area of water, Lower Pond, which is to your right, your path splits into forks, one green path veering away to the left, the other veering immediately half right; it is this latter path you need, the path in fact proceeding clearly in roughly the same direction as previously and rising gently, going forward to arrive at a car park. There's a pillar that looks like a trig point alongside the path just before you enter the car park, although it's not marked on maps or shown on the trig points website as such. Pass through the car park to arrive at the A283, turning left and following this road for a quarter of a mile to Limbo Farm which is on the right, and immediately opposite which is a signed footpath heading west through a gate. Take this path, actually a wide track, which passes over two crossing tracks (one almost immediately), then at the third crossing track, a major path crossroads, you need to turn right. It's now straightforward walking as you head just west of north uphill, out of the woodland, and having climbed to the top of the rise you can enjoy excellent views towards Black Down. You pass the fine buildings of Stagpark Farm which you can see clearly down to your left, and reach what is a crossroads of metalled tracks. You're warned of a bull in the field ahead, but in fact you need to turn right(eastwards) here along a clear metalled track which soon bends right; as it does so, you bear left along a fainter track towards woodland and beside a field. Just before you reach the woods, turn right to follow the field edge round, keeping to your left firstly woodland, then a gate (which you pass without going through), then a hedge. It's not a designated right of way, but access presents no problems. The Stagpark Farm trig point is half hidden in the hedge just a few yards after the gate, but although the setting of the trig point is disappointing, the views and the surroundings are most pleasant. Continue round the field edge to arrive back at the clear metalled track which you now follow just north of east, back to the A283 at Colhook; turn left along this road for half a mile, passing the welcome Flower Bowl garage which offers refreshment opportunity, then turn right at the signed Blackwool Farm turning and follow the farm approach road briefly. Shortly you reach a signed bridleway going off to the left, and you follow this bridleway in a northerly direction through the woods, ignoring a path soon going off to the right and, just beyond a field which you see immediately to the right, ignoring a further path going off to the right. Very soon a signpost reassures you and you go forward to reach a road. Turn right then almost immediately left onto a lane going past houses, but after 100 yards or so, bear left to join a bridlepath which heads fractionally west of north through the woods again. You soon go over a crossroads of paths and now you need to ensure you keep to the path and observe the signposts, ignoring crossing tracks and descending to a stream.

The Peacock's Farm trig point completely submerged by hedge!

The Black Down trig point in spring sunshine

The going here can get exceedingly muddy. The bridlepath swings in a more north-westerly direction and becomes much better defined, crossing a metalled track and entering thicker woodland, going forward to reach, in just over a quarter of a mile, a signed crossroads of public footpaths where you turn right. Now walk north-eastwards along an excellent path, in a few hundred yards arriving at a further path crossroads; go over that and almost immediately you will reach the edge of the woodland+ with a track leading just north of east towards a radio beacon. Bear right to follow this track to the beacon, and immediately beyond the beacon bear right alongside the hedge to reach the Peacock's Farm trig point which once more is hidden in the hedge just beside the beacon itself. There are beautiful views to the surrounding countryside. Retrace your steps to the point marked + above, bearing right onto the main track which now veers just west of north to arrive at a junction with a metalled road at Peacock's Farm. Turn left to follow this metalled road which in just over a quarter of a mile swings sharply right; turn right with the road then bear left onto a signed footpath which heads westwards, parallel with the road but along the edge of a field below it. You cross a stile and go forward to enter the churchyard of Northchapel church, passing the church and almost immediately arriving at the A283 for what will be the last time on this walk! Turn left to follow the road past the village store, a most useful amenity, then very shortly beyond the store turn right onto the signed Hillgrove road which soon bends left and proceeds pleasantly to the hamlet of Hillgrove. You arrive at a road junction at which you turn right then bear immediately left onto a signed footpath, entering a field and following it south-westwards downhill, aiming for a stile at the edge of woodland. Cross the stile to continue along the path through the wood, veering just north of west and descending to a charming footbridge, then rising again beyond the bridge and, going through the trees, passing a little lake which is to your right. You shortly emerge from the woods and now follow the left-hand field edge in a westerly direction, the path reasonably well defined and signposted, and commanding good views of Black Down ahead. You now veer south-westwards, ignoring a path going off to the right, and enter a wooded area, your path suddenly dropping quite dramatically to a footbridge in the wood, then rising steeply. Emerge from the wood and into a field, but don't take what looks like a clear path straight ahead, rather bearing half right, aiming for and passing over a stile across the field. You pass a footpath fingerpost with arrows pointing ahead and left, then almost immediately you reach another fingerpost with arrows pointing ahead and right. Here you turn right and now climb quite steeply through the field to reach the buildings of Hobstevens, negotiating first a stile then an insulated electric fence crossing to arrive at the driveway that in turn leads you to the road. Bear right onto the road then almost immediately left onto a very narrow road that snakes uphill, and in roughly three quarters of a mile you arrive at a T-junction, a prominent sign saying FERNDEN LANE, and a small parking area to your left. DON'T take the bridleway heading sharply right (north) from here but turn half right to join a clear footpath heading westwards away from the road into the woods and climbing steeply. It's a long zigzag climb but eventually you arrive at the topograph and viewing seat of Black Down, with quite magnificent views. Take the path going up from the right (east) side of the topograph, the path now proceeding to the very top of Black Down and widening out; continue along this path, ignoring paths coming in from the left, and keeping the woodland/escarpment edge just to the right. Shortly beyond the second path coming from the left, you reach a fingerpost* with the bridleway signed forward and backward, and there may after wet weather be a little pond just to the right. Turn left here onto a signed path which rises gently; just beyond the top of the rise, as it starts to drop, turn right onto a narrow path which keeps to the topmost ground and arrives at the Black Down trig point from which the views through the trees are magnificent. Retrace your steps to the fingerpost asterisked above and bear left along the bridlepath, ignoring turnings off to the left but continuing as signed and joining up with the Sussex Border Path. The views through the trees to the right remain very good. You descend with the Sussex Border Path to Tennyson's Lane, turning left to follow this for just over a mile to a T-junction with Chase Lane, here turning right then first left into Scotland Lane. Just beyond Denbigh Road on the right is a signed footpath which you follow all the way down to the B2131 Petworth Road, turning left here and then very shortly right to arrive in the delightful centre of Haslemere. There's a bus stop close to the museum.

3 Midhurst SU881223 EASY.

Regular buses(SC) serving Midhurst from Chichester, Haslemere and Pulborough. 1.5 miles. R Midhurst (P,C,S).

From the bus stand in North Street at Midhurst, cross straight over North Street into Lambert's Lane and follow it away from North Street to a very sharp bend. On the bend follow the signed path with the legend "New Lipchis Way" away from Lambert's Lane heading north-westwards along a left-hand field edge. You swing in a more westerly direction, arriving at a field boundary* with woods up to the right, where the New Lipchis Way is signed going off to the left. Carry straight on to the next field boundary and turn right immediately beyond it to follow the boundary hedge uphill(northwards). The trig point is hidden rather coyly in the hedge, with good views to the surrounding countryside. Return to the field boundary asterisked above and follow the New Lipchis Way signed path southwards uphill to reach a T-junction with June Lane. Turn left to follow June Lane to a T-junction with North Street in the centre of Midhurst.

4 Ambersham Common SU915195 MODERATE.

Regular buses(SC) serving Midhurst from Chichester, Haslemere and Pulborough. 6 miles. R Midhurst (P,C,S).

This walk starts, like walk 3, at the North Street bus stand in Midhurst. Make your way eastwards from the bus stand on a signed path along the left-hand side of the car park heading for the Cowdray Ruins. The original Cowdray House was developed in the 16th century but much of it was destroyed by fire in 1793. In due course you arrive at the river; as you approach it, don't cross the bridge but turn right to follow an attractive riverside path. The path bends to the right, then at the next junction of paths a few yards beyond you take the path to the left, continuing to follow the river in the shade of trees. You arrive at an open area, going forward to cross a bridge over a tributary stream, then immediately beyond the bridge turn left onto a path that rises sharply. Keep to this very pretty woodland path which becomes metalled and arrives at a junction with the West Lavington-Ambersham road which you join, continuing in the same direction. Walk on past the twin farmsteads of Great Todham and Little Todham then, a little way beyond the latter, bear left onto a signed footpath which goes initially parallel with the road, then branches off to the left. You descend and proceed parallel with the Rother, dropping down to walk beside it and arriving at the road at Ambersham Bridge; turn right onto the road and follow it to South Ambersham, then, continuing along the road, climb away from the valley. You pass under the old Petworth-Midhurst railway, noting the remains of the bridge, and shortly beyond the bridge remains you

The Ambersham Common trig point - an oasis in the heather

turn left onto a signed path. This goes round the left side of a small car park, then bears sharp left and climbs, arriving at a junction of paths, now on the very attractive heaths of Ambersham Common. Turn hard left onto a path that could be very soggy in wet weather; this arrives at a T-junction with a better path, and the trig point can be seen a few yards ahead. The views from the trig point are delightful, with Ambersham Common providing superb surroundings. Retrace your steps to the road but now go straight across onto an opposite path, very soon reaching a junction of tracks and bearing right onto a track that takes you to the old railway line. Turn left onto the line and follow it to enjoy a lovely walk with beautiful views. Pass under a fine overbridge, then turn right at the next crossroads of paths; soon you reach a T-junction of paths and bear left onto a path that proceeds attractively through open countryside then in the shade of woodland. At a sharp right bend continue ahead on a signed path in the same direction as that you've been following, walking uphill then steeply down. Turn right at the T-junction at the foot of the hill and go forward to a crossroads; go straight over the crossroads onto a road that takes you in just under a mile into Midhurst. At the T-junction at the end of the road turn right onto a road that passes a pond then goes gently uphill with shops to the left and a large church to the right. The road descends and bends left, arriving at a T-junction with North Street, and you now turn right to follow North Street back to the bus station.

5 Halfway Bridge SU934224 EASY.

Regular buses(SC) serving Halfway Bridge on Worthing-Pulborough-Midhurst route. 2.5 miles. R Halfway Bridge (P), Lodsworth (P).

From the bus stop on the north side of the A272 at Halfway Bridge between Midhurst and Petworth, walk a few yards in the Petworth direction then turn left onto a minor road which snakes round the side of the popular Halfway Bridge Inn and passes over a river, a tributary of the nearby Rother. The road swings from north-east to south-east and heads back towards the A272 but before arriving at the A272 you turn left onto a signed path with fields on both sides. You arrive at a large house just to the left of the path at the edge of woodland, and here* turn right to climb a grassy bank that takes you to a trig point from which there are lovely views to the South Downs and the extensive woodland to the north-east of Midhurst. If you were pushed for time you could just walk back the way you came, but for a more interesting walk retrace your steps to the point asterisked above and now turn right to follow a signed path just east of north into the woods. You now enjoy a lovely woodland walk, the ground falling away dramatically to the left down to the river. You pass a fingerpost with a yellow arrow, but then when you arrive at a fingerpost with a blue arrow you turn left to follow a bridleway downhill through the woods, cross a bridge over the river then veer from north-west to

The weatherbeaten Halfway Bridge trig point

westwards along a clear path uphill through fields. Just short of the houses, on the edge of the village of Lodsworth, you veer left along the path and go forward to join a metalled lane. The lane veers right, and passes the very attractive Lodsworth Church with its fine Millennium tapestry. Just beyond the lychgate, turn left onto a lane and follow it, going forward to join a very good path with fine views to the downs ahead. Keep to the path which descends to a T-junction with the road close to the Halfway Bridge Inn. You have come full circle. Turn right to ascend to the A272 and the bus stop close by.

6 Trotton Common SU845222 MODERATE.

Regular buses(CL Mon-Sat, SC Sun) serving Trotton on Midhurst-Petersfield route. 3 miles. R Trotton (P).

The walk starts at the A272 bridge crossing of the River Rother just east of the centre of Trotton, the crossing controlled by traffic lights. Walk beside the A272 east from the bridge then take the first right turn signposted Dumpford. Pass the pub which is to your left and continue briefly along the road, then just before the road swings right, westwards, bear left along a signed bridleway heading south-east, marked SERPENTS TRAIL - be careful because there appear to be two forked paths here, and you need the left-hand one. The path continues very pleasantly south-eastwards with lovely views to the left across Trotton Common. In a little under half a mile, having steadily gained height, you reach a junction of paths with two tracks going off to the left; don't turn hard left but take the gentler left turn and follow this track heading across the common. You arrive at another junction with the Serpents Trail going off to the right, downhill, but although this looks the more attractive path you should not bear right onto it but rather stay on the same path, maintaining height. You veer from north-east to just east of north and cross over a well-defined track, your path rather less clearly defined, and you'll see the trig point half-hidden in bushes to the left. There are good views across the common to the South Downs escarpment. Return to the path and continue just east of north downhill, veering sharply right and then left to reach the A272; cross over with care, bear left along the roadside briefly and turn first right on to a metalled side road. The road soon bends sharp left but you need to go straight ahead onto a signed path heading northwards, past buildings which are to your left then uphill along a right-hand field edge. You reach a T-junction of paths at the end of the field, with woods behind, and here you turn left and proceed westwards keeping woodland to your right and fields to your left. In due course the woodland to the right relents, and you now descend to cross a narrow footbridge and arrive at a road. Turn left to follow the road briefly, then as it bends left in a couple of hundred yards you bear right onto a signed footpath which initially follows a right-hand field edge then crosses into the field to the right and follows the left edge of that one, keeping the most attractive Rother valley to

Daughter Jennifer and Chester resting beside the Trotton Common trig point

the right. Proceeding south-westwards, you drop down to pass through an area of woodland and a small area of meadow, now on the valley floor, and go forward to reach the A272. Turn right to arrive back at the bridge where you began.

7 Combe Hill, Near Hill Brow SU798260 STRENUOUS IN PLACES.
Regular trains(OPERATED BY SOUTH WEST TRAINS) serving Liss on Petersfield-Haslemere line; regular buses(SC) serving Hill Brow on Petersfield-Liss Forest route. 2.5 miles. R Hill Brow (P).

The walk starts at the pub in the village of Hill Brow on the B2070(old A3) between Petersfield and Rake; if there are no convenient buses to Hill Brow it's a 1-mile walk to here from Liss station via the B3006(turn left out of the station onto Station Road then bear very shortly right into Hill Brow Road which takes you to the B2070 by the pub). From the pub at Hill Brow, head south-eastwards along the road signed for Rogate, then just beyond the Knowles Meadow estate bear left onto the road signed for Milland,

Linch and Fernhurst. The road goes steeply downhill and soon bends left, proceeding north-eastwards in a straight line; shortly bear right onto a signed footpath with the Serpents Trail logo. Follow this path eastwards through delightful woodland for just under half a mile, until you pass beneath overhead wires crossing the path in a north-westerly - south-easterly direction. Shortly after passing under these wires fencing starts on the left; immediately it does so bear right off the path and climb the bank on a crude path that goes extremely steeply up the hillside. There are numerous paths, some clearer than others, but as you gain height you need to veer right so that you're under the overhead wires again, and then proceed south-eastwards uphill with the wires directly underneath you all the while. You cross a clear path and continue on a thin path to pass through a gap in a fence separating the thicker woodland from an area of grass with younger trees. Having passed the gap, look half right and you will see a mast ahead of you. Make as if to head for the mast along a green path between the trees, and almost at once you'll arrive at the Combe Hill trig point, half concealed in vegetation and at the time of writing, uprooted. The views aren't great but the surrounding woodland is certainly attractive. In theory you could proceed due south from the trig point and pass through another gap in fencing to shortly reach the Hill Brow-Rogate road, turning right and following the road back to Hill Brow. Or you could retrace your steps to Hill Brow.

The distinctly precarious-looking Combe Hill trig point

8 Forestside SU769121 EASY.

Regular buses(CL) serving West Marden on Chichester-Petersfield route. 3 miles. R West Marden (P).

From the centre of the pretty village of West Marden follow the signed minor road south-westwards for just over a mile to Forestside, in due course arriving at the sharp corner at the east end of the Forestside village street. Bear left to join a signed path that proceeds just west of south from this corner, heading across a field to reach an area of woodland and passing a path coming from the right. Enter the woodland and shortly bear left onto another signed path that proceeds south-eastwards along the left-hand edge of the wood, then emerges into open country but keeping a field boundary to the left. You rise gently and are able to see and use one of the gaps in the hedge to access the trig point across the field (there is no designated right of way through the field so you should ideally seek permission; please refer to introductory notes). The views are not panoramic, but the countryside surrounding the trig point is certainly very attractive. Rejoin the path and continue along it, swinging south-eastwards to reach the buildings of Broadreed Farm and go forward to a T-junction with a metalled lane; bear left onto the lane and proceed to the woodland, continuing straight on, ignoring paths going off right and left. The lane bends left and descends north-westwards through the woods to reach Oldhouse Lane. To reach West Marden you could cross the road to join a path that contours the hillside to reach the village; alternatively turn right onto the road and then left at the next junction to arrive at West Marden.

9 Ladyholt Park SU753160 MODERATE.

Regular buses(CL) serving Littlegreen School on Chichester-Petersfield route. 3 miles. R none.

From the entrance gates of Littlegreen School on the B2146 Funtington-Harting road between Compton and Uppark, cross over and take the minor road turning signposted Finchdean, heading south-westwards. Very shortly fork right onto a metalled lane which goes first uphill then drops to the buildings of Cowdown Farm. Pass through the farm complex then continue just south of west on what's signposted as a "soft road route to Chalton." You climb gently in the shade of woodland - it is lovely walking, especially in the spring - and in just under half a mile reach a signed crossroads junction with a bridleway. Turn right to follow the bridleway gently uphill through a field, just west of north, to reach a patch of woodland. Beyond the woodland the path (contrary to the signpost at the time of writing) veers just east of north on a right-hand field edge, then soon veers sharply left along the field edge keeping a fence to the right. (Some OS maps

The Ladyholt Park trig point, among the cow parsley in May

show a slightly different course here). Climb up to another footpath junction* but don't turn hard right as the sign seems to indicate; veer very gently right and, aiming for a tall tree ahead, proceed along the field boundary to reach the trig point. It is impressively sited, with lovely views in all directions, the buildings of Ditcham Park School very prominent to the north-west. Retrace your steps to the signed path junction asterisked above and now turn left (north-east) along a lovely clear path that follows the hilltop through Ladyholt Park, allowing excellent views including Uppark House to the north-east. You are signed left then almost immediately right, and descend to a T-junction with a driveway. Turn right to follow the driveway past the buildings of Eckensfield, a couple of hundred yards beyond which the driveway veers sharp right then shortly left; as it veers left, bear right onto a signed footpath that goes south across the field. You pass through a patch of woodland via 2 squeeze stiles then follow a path south-eastwards across the next field to arrive at the metalled approach lane to Cowdown Farm, thus completing the circle. Turn left to follow the lane downhill to the T-junction with the Finchdean road, turning left here to arrive back at Littlegreen School.

10 Court Hill/Heyshott Down SU897137/900166

MODERATE, STRENUOUS IN PLACES.

Regular buses(SC) serving Singleton and Cocking on Chichester-Midhurst route. 6.5 miles maximum, 5 miles minimum. R Singleton (P,C,S), Cocking (P,C,S - just off route).

This walk incorporates a trig point that is just off the South Downs Way and for which there's a separate description in the South Downs Way section. PLEASE NOTE THAT FROM THE DOUBLE-ASTERISKED POINT TO THE COURT HILL TRIG POINT AND BACK THERE IS NO PUBLIC RIGHT OF ACCESS AT ALL AND A NUMBER OF GATES AND FENCES (SOME OF WHICH ARE OF BARBED WIRE) NEED TO BE SURMOUNTED. PLEASE REFER TO MY INTRODUCTORY NOTES. From the sharp bend of the main road in the centre of the pretty village of Singleton, bear eastwards along the road for Charlton and East Dean, soon swinging left to head away from the village centre. Continue eastwards along this road beside the winterbourne River Lavant for a little over half a mile to Charlton; just as you enter the village, there is a crossroads with North Lane, an unmade-up farm road, going off to the left, and a little car park on the corner. Bear left up North Lane and follow it for about half a mile until you reach a track going off to the right, North Lane itself swinging left(north-westwards)* and a gated path signed straight ahead. Turn right and **immediately right again through a gate into a field, then follow the field uphill along

The lofty but strictly private Court Hill trig point

the left-hand field boundary, just south of east. Go through the gate at the next field boundary, then walk diagonally across the next field, heading uphill and aiming just left of the very top right-hand corner with a patch of woodland immediately beyond. Looking eastwards from the top of the field, you'll see another field with the ground rising still further, and you need to surmount two fences to get into this field, aiming for the highest ground and just to the right of the trees. There's then another fence which you have to surmount to reach the Court Hill trig point, from which there are really lovely views southwards to the Lavant valley and Goodwood. Now retrace your steps all the way back to the single-asterisked point above(where North Lane swings north-westwards). Although obviously you could just return to Charlton and Singleton the same way, the suggested walk - now using legitimate public rights of way throughout - continues up North Lane, which having swung north-westwards veers right and heads for a large area of forest. Just as the lane is about to enter the forest it reaches a crossroads of footpaths where you turn left, into the forest itself(don't be tempted along the track that forks immediately left from here along the forest edge). Very soon you'll reach a T-junction with a much wider track; turn left and follow it north-westwards in a dead straight line, gaining height all the time. At length you arrive not only on the top of the hill but at the northern edge of the woods where your path ends at a T-junction with the South Downs Way, and you turn right now to follow the South Downs Way. You pass over a signed bridleway junction, beyond which you continue eastwards on a clear straight path with woodland immediately to your right and open fields separating you from the woods of Heyshott Down to the left. A couple of hundred yards beyond the signed bridleway junction you come to a signed footpath junction; turn left(north-east) along the footpath and rise slightly to reach the Heyshott Down trig point which is actually on this path and from which there are lovely views northwards to the beautiful countryside north of Midhurst. Return to the footpath junction and turn right to follow the South Downs Way as signposted, heading just south then just north of west, downhill, to arrive at Cocking Hill car park and bus stop with buses available back to Singleton and Chichester and northwards to Midhurst. By turning right (northwards) onto the main A286 road you will soon reach the pretty village of Cocking which boasts a good range of refreshment opportunities.

11 Bow Hill/Oldwick Farm SU824112/840073 STRENUOUS.

Regular buses(CL) serving Walderton on Chichester-Petersfield route; regular trains from Chichester to Brighton, Horsham and Portsmouth; there are also excellent bus links from Chichester. 9 miles. R Walderton (P), Stoughton (P), Oldwick (C), Chichester (P,C,S).

If you're reliant on public transport you'll need to start at the B2146 by Walderton and

The Bow Hill trig point, dwarfed by the surrounding vegetation

follow the road running north-eastwards to Stoughton from the B2146. Proceed along the road through the village of Stoughton past the little green and the very popular pub, then as the road bends slightly left a little beyond the pub, bear right onto the signed bridleway which soon veers left and proceeds clearly, fractionally north of east. You follow this bridleway, part of the Monarch's Way long distance footpath, past some farm buildings then begin to climb, and proceed quite steeply uphill onto Stoughton Down. The views back down to Stoughton and beyond are very good. Having gained the brow of the hill at the edge of the woods, about a mile from Stoughton, you reach a crossroads of paths; turn right onto the bridleway heading just east of south, but almost immediately look out for and take a signed bridleway forking left off the main track. This is very easily missed, so take care! The signed bridleway, significantly narrower than the main track you have left, proceeds uphill through the woods; ignoring a bridleway turning to the right, you keep climbing and reach what is obviously the brow of the hill. Just beyond the brow you reach another crossroads of paths*, now on Bow Hill, and at this crossroads you turn right and proceed south-westwards along a clear path. Just before this path swings to the right(westwards) there's a narrow path going off to the right which takes you to the Bow Hill trig point in a clearing, the views from the trig point sadly being nonexistent. Return the few steps to the main path** and you now have a choice. If you want to return to Walderton on effectively a circular tour, turn right and follow the main path which as stated above swings westwards and very soon arrives at the extraordinary green hillocks known as the Devil's Humps, with views which are some of the finest in West Sussex. Aim for the top of the far "hump" and leave it by dropping down to the bridlepath on its far (north-west) side (this bridlepath running parallel to the one you used to reach the humps). Turn left to follow the bridlepath south-westwards through the woods, maintaining height, then emerge from the woods and, keeping to the path, you veer north-westwards and drop down very steeply to arrive back at Stoughton. Turn left to follow the road back to Walderton. To continue to the

West Stoke trig point, though, turn left at the point double-asterisked above and retrace your steps to the crossroads single-asterisked above; turn right at this crossroads and follow the path, soon emerging from the woods and enjoying a fantastic view of Chichester and its cathedral, and the surrounding countryside and coast. Descend steeply through fields to reach a crossroads of paths, going straight over and then climbing again. Proceeding just south of the woodland of Stoke Clump, you then gently descend to a junction with a road; turn right to follow the road briefly but almost immediately turn left into West Stoke Road. Continue along it until you reach on your left the attractive flint-built Oldwick Farm complex, a business park including a restaurant/cafe at the time of writing. Immediately opposite the complex, turn right along a farm track, the track heading south-west towards a wood, but just before you reach the trees, turn right along the left-hand field edge and in a few yards you'll see the Oldwick Farm trig point in the edge of the trees on the left. It may be obscured by vegetation so don't be surprised if you fail to see it at first! Retrace your steps to the complex and turn right to continue along West Stoke Road to a crossroads, going straight over and following the road on to a junction with Old Broyle Road, here turning left and following Old Broyle Road to the Northgate roundabout. Turn left to pass St Paul's Church and then cross over the A286, swinging right to pass a car park entrance and going under the subway, then, emerging from the subway, take the next left into North Street and the centre of Chichester.

12 Lavant/The Trundle SU866080/877111 STRENUOUS.

Regular buses(SC) serving Lavant on Chichester-Midhurst route. 6 miles. R Lavant (P).

Leaving the bus at the bus stop by the Earl of March pub on the main street in Lavant, walk up the main road (in the Midhurst direction) for a few yards, soon turning hard right down Sheepwash Lane. To your left is the picturesque River Lavant, which usually flows in the early months of the year unless the winter is dry. At the T-junction with Pook Lane turn left, immediately crossing the bridge over the river; to your left is St Mary's Church, with a nave and west doorway that both date back to the 12th century. More or less opposite the church turn right into Fordwater Road and follow it south-eastwards for a little over a quarter of a mile. The road bends sharply left; follow it round and you will soon see the Lavant trig point on the left-hand side, perched on the bank. Retrace your steps along Fordwater Road to the T-junction with Pook Lane and this time turn right to follow the lane heading north-eastwards through the village of East Lavant. As the road bends to head eastwards, turn left onto Chalkpit Lane, a wide but very uneven track, and follow it uphill; it's quite a long slog of nearly 2 miles but the views get better and better as you climb. Eventually you reach the crest of the hill and a footpath junction* by a car park at the south-east corner of a large patch of woodland. Bear right and now follow a very clear path uphill aiming for the masts atop the hillfort known as the Trundle, one of the finest viewpoints in Sussex with magnificent views to Chichester, the coastline, the Channel and even the Isle of Wight. When you reach the fort you can join a path that goes all the way round the perimeter and can clearly see the Trundle trig point at the centre. Retrace your steps down to the footpath junction asterisked above and go straight over to join a path heading just west of south, veering slightly away from the woodland(don't join the path going into the woods). Your path quickly loses height and drops steeply downhill, veering in a more south-westerly direction to meet a crossroads of paths. Turn left here onto a path which proceeds just west of south down the hillside to the valley bottom, then swings just east of south to follow close to the Centurion Way - the course of the old Chichester-Midhurst railway - and the river Lavant. The path arrives at a T-junction with Sheepwash Lane. Turn right onto Sheepwash Lane to return to the start of the walk.

13 Chichester SU880039 EASY.
Regular buses(SC) serving Whyke Road on Chichester-Selsey route. 2.5 miles. R Chichester (P,C,S).

This walk starts from the very pleasant Crown Inn on the west side of Whyke Road, Chichester, a little way south of the level crossing gates; the nearest bus stop is at the junction of Whyke Road and Willowbed Drive and the Crown is reached by walking northwards up Whyke Road for 100 yards or so. The dull bit of this walk comes first as you head eastwards along Quarry Lane which goes off from Whyke Road more or less opposite the Crown. You pass along Quarry Lane and through its large industrial estate; as the road bends sharply left you continue straight on along the signed South Coast Cycle Route to reach the roundabout where the A27 meets the A259. Bear right to cross the impressive footbridge over the A27 and descend to Vinnetrow Road. Turn right to briefly follow Vinnetrow Road southwards, very soon passing a public footpath sign* which is to your right; just beyond the sign, cross the road and make your way into the field which although not fenced has no public right of way into it, so please refer to my introductory notes. Having entered the field, bear right and follow the right-hand field edge round, swinging east. Continue east and go forward to a line of trees coming in from the right, the trig point now visible at the left (north) end of the trees; the surroundings, it has to be said, aren't hugely appealing but you can see the hills to the north-east of Chichester in the background. Retrace your steps to the public footpath sign asterisked above, and follow the path as directed by the sign, just west of south, with a succession of lakes to your left. Look out for when the last lake ends on the left and gives way to fields; at this point there's a footpath sign, with a house called

Ferndale immediately adjacent, and you turn hard right onto this signed path, heading north-westwards with lakes on both sides including Ivy Lake, a nature reserve, on the right. After a walk on what has been a delightful path, you reach a T-junction with the B2145, turning right and following alongside it northwards to a roundabout junction with the A27. Cross very carefully using the footpath signs as shown and continue northwards up Whyke Road to arrive back at the Crown where you deserve a drink!

14 St Wilfrid's Chapel SZ868957 EASY.
Regular buses(SC) serving Ferry Corner on Chichester-Selsey route. 2.5 miles. R none.

Leaving the bus from Chichester at the small Ferry Gate industrial estate just beyond Ferry Corner on the B2145 Chichester-Selsey road, bear left onto a signed footpath heading just north of east, away from the B2145 just beyond the estate. The footpath is open and very clear, and seemingly wide enough to accommodate vehicles. After a few hundred yards it swings left then shortly right, the way ahead still obvious, but take care to bear right at the path junction that shortly follows, although this is well signposted. Shortly after the swing to the right, you veer to the left and now continue slightly south of east, in the shade of trees; before long, however, you veer southwards and the

The winter sunshine gives a long shadow to the St Wilfrid's Chapel trig point

countryside opens up splendidly to the left, providing superb views across Pagham Harbour to Bognor Regis. Having veered south, look to your right and you will see the trig point on this walk in the middle of the field. There appears to be no difficulty of access into the field but there isn't a designated right of way across it(please refer to my introductory notes). Having visited the trig point, part of the Ordnance Survey GPS network, you could just retrace your steps to the B2145 and the bus back. However, much to be preferred is to continue southwards along the path, soon arriving at the road in the hamlet of Church Norton, and here you turn left to follow this road to the car park at St Wilfrid's Chapel. The chapel, which is well worth a small detour, dates from the 13th century and was once much larger than it is today; however, in 1864 all but the chancel of the building was removed to St Peter's in Selsey nearby for the convenience of residents. The chancel, which by ecclesiastical law couldn't be removed, was restored in 1905. Walk through the car park and down to the shore, passing The Mound, an earthwork that is thought to be a Roman coastal defence fort. On reaching the shore bear left to follow a shoreside path alongside Pagham Harbour which is now a nature reserve most noteworthy for being a visiting place and breeding ground for the little tern, one of Britain's rarest breeding sea birds. The going is somewhat slippery in places, but soon you reach a proper embankment path, providing easier walking, and you're able to stay on the embankment virtually all the way back to the B2145. When you reach the road, turn left onto it and follow it, soon reaching the industrial complex with bus stops clearly marked on both sides of the road.

15 Almodington SZ834973 EASY.
Regular buses(SC) serving Pagham Harbour Nature Reserve on Chichester-Selsey route. 4 miles. R none.

The walk starts at the Pagham Harbour Nature Reserve car park on the B2145 just south of Sidlesham. Turn right out of the car park and walk very briefly up the B2145 northwards but almost at once turn left onto a signed path which initially is a metalled lane, heading south-westwards. Where the metalled lane turns sharp left, southwards, continue south-westwards as before along the signed grassy path, very soon reaching a path fork. Bear right (westwards) here along an obvious path, soon kinking left then right, aiming for the buildings of Oakhurst Farm. The path veers left, south-westwards, to arrive at a T-junction with the road, and you turn right along the road, keeping Oakhurst Farm on your right. The road soon bends right and proceeds just west of north, then shortly, opposite the house marked on larger-scale OS maps as Veriwell, bear left onto a signed path that proceeds north-westwards through fields. The course on the ground isn't always obvious, but if you keep looking ahead to the field boundaries the way ahead should be clear and in half a mile or so you'll arrive at a road on a right-

Assorted vegetation laps at the Almodington trig point

angled bend. Turn left and very shortly right up a concrete slipway that leads to a very large shed, keeping the Easton Farm complex to your left. Pass to the left of the shed to arrive at a field, then turn left to follow the field edge to the field boundary, and turn sharp right to follow a farm track heading north-eastwards on the left(west) side of the boundary. In a couple of hundred yards you'll reach the trig point which nestles in long grass to the left of the track. The surroundings are unremarkable, with flat fields on all sides and the nurseries of Almodington a short way to the west. Beyond the trig point, continue along the track to reach a T-junction with a signed path; turn right to follow this path, a nice clear green strip with a field boundary immediately to the left. Continue south-eastwards on this path, passing just to the left of Oldhouse Farm Cottages, arriving at a metalled lane, then go south-eastwards along this lane to a T-junction with a road. Turn left to follow the road north-eastwards to a T-junction with the Sidlesham-Highleigh road, then turn right to follow this road past a primary school. The road, Keynor Lane, bends sharply right and straightens, and you then need to take the second right turn, Chalk Lane. Follow it just west of south then just east of south past various nurseries and industrial units, then at the bottom when the lane does a 90-degree right turn, you go forward a little then left(eastwards) along a signed path which emerges at a metalled turning area. Turn right here along a minor road that brings you back to the B2145 onto which you turn right once more, following this road back to the nature reserve car park.

16 Merston SU899029 EASY.

Regular buses(SC) serving Merston Corner on Chichester - Bognor Regis - Littlehampton route. 1 mile. R none.

From the Merston Corner bus stop at the junction of the A259 Bognor-Chichester road with the minor road signposted Merston, follow this minor road into the tiny village of Merston just over a quarter of a mile away. When reaching the village centre, such as it is, the road bends sharply left, then right, then right again; on the second right-hand bend, there's a signed footpath going off to the left along a farm lane. Walk along the lane to a sharp right-hand bend immediately beyond which you bear left into a field. Follow the left-hand field edge, soon veering right - eastwards - and now proceed eastwards across to the very far side of the field; although it's not a designated right of way, access is no problem. Having reached the far side, turn left to follow the right-hand field edge, keeping a stream to your right, and shortly you'll see the trig point in the bushes on the right-hand side. Curiously the trig point doesn't show on the most recent OS Explorer map! You could either retrace your steps to the start, detouring when you get back to the road and following it south-westwards to explore the very pretty Merston Church, or, as a short cut, you could continue along the right-hand field edge from the trig point to the A259, bearing left to follow beside the A259 to return to the bus stop. It's safer to use the cycle path on the other side of this very busy road.

16A Lidsey SU930039

All current OS maps at the time of writing show a trig point at Lidsey, just off a footpath running southwards from Park Farm a little west of the twin villages of Westergate and Woodgate on the A29 between Fontwell (junction with A27) and Bognor Regis. However, the land on which this trig point supposedly stands is now part of the Lidsey Landfill site, the marked footpath has been rerouted, and the landfill site is now strictly out of bounds. Furthermore, Ian Stark, the site manager, advises me that the trig point itself has been removed.

17 Shripney SU930023 EASY.

Regular buses(SC) serving Robin Hood Inn on Bognor Regis-Walberton route. 1 mile. R Shripney (P).

This is an ideal pre/post-pub lunch walk! From the Robin Hood Inn on the A29 at

Shripney on the outskirts of Bognor Regis, cross the A29 carefully and turn right, walking northwards for a few yards then turning left onto a signed path along a left-hand field edge; turn sharp left as signposted in a couple of hundred yards and walk southwards along a metalled drive past a caravan park which is to your left. At the end turn right onto the road* then as it very shortly bends left, turn right onto the Manor Farm driveway and head north-westwards along it. You pass more caravans which are to your left, then beyond the caravans continue with a field to your left, soon reaching a field boundary/ditch on your left. Immediately beyond the ditch turn left along the left-hand field edge, keeping the ditch hard to your left; you'll see the trig point very shortly on your left, looking down into the ditch! The surroundings aren't that special but there are good views northwards to the Downs. You could simply retrace your steps but for a bit of variety, continue on the road past the junction asterisked above then just beyond the white-painted Shripney House a few yards further on, turn left onto a signed gravel path. It shortly bends sharp right, then left, then right again to arrive at the A29, and it just remains for you to turn left and walk back up the A29 to the pub.

18 Flansham/Yapton SU953017/983017 MODERATE.
Regular buses(SC) serving Yapton on Chichester-Bognor Regis-Littlehampton route. 5 miles. R Yapton (P,S).

Your walk starts at Bilsham Road in Yapton at the junction with Loveys Road. Walk briefly south-westwards (away from the village centre) along Bilsham Road and turn right into Mill View Road. Turn right at the end into The Millers, then just past number 24 turn left along a metalled path in front of houses, going forward along an obvious signed path north-westwards beside a left-hand field edge. You reach a T-junction of paths at the top end; go up to the signpost and turn left here to walk south-westwards along the signed path, then shortly bear right, again as signposted, north-westwards to reach Drove Lane. There are good views to Barnham Windmill across the fields to the right, and you may also see Butlins across to the left! Turn left at the path end into Drove Lane and follow what is a clear farm track south-westwards through the farm complex, then continue along the track which in due course swings right at a gate. Don't swing right with it but continue south-westwards on a signed path, passing another signed path going off to the left,* then shortly beyond that you go over a footbridge, Weststone Bridge. Keep on the path south-westwards under the pylons then shortly a signed path goes off to the right. You need to take this path which heads westwards on a left-hand field edge, going forward into a second field, passing the fine buildings of Hoe Farm(just north-west of the village of Flansham) which are on the left, and reaching a T-junction of paths; turn left here and in a few yards you'll see the Flansham trig point tucked in vegetation on the right at what is another path junction. Retrace

Pointing the way away from the Flansham trig point

your steps via Weststone Bridge to the path asterisked above. Turn right to follow it south-east along a left-hand field edge, then hard left as signed to proceed north-east along another left-hand field edge, arriving at the far west end of Bilsham Lane. Turn right to follow this lane just south of east all the way to Bilsham Road, passing the delightful buildings of Old Bilsham Farm and Bilsham Manor. Turn left on reaching

Bilsham Road and then in a couple of hundred yards turn right onto a signed path heading just south of east. It's a very obvious path which you follow all the way to a junction with a wide track where there's a footpath sign pointing left and right** and a large PRIVATE PROPERTY notice to the right. Turn right here then very shortly right as signed (ahead is private) along a narrow path heading southwards through a field to arrive at a footbridge, the main A259 just ahead. Don't cross the footbridge but bear left just before it along the right-hand field edge with a stream to your right, and in a few yards you'll reach the

A bramble archway over the Yapton trig point   Yapton trig point. Despite the traffic noise the surroundings are very pleasant if a little overgrown. Retrace your steps to the double-asterisked footpath sign and this time continue straight on north-westwards as directed by the sign along a clear if narrow path that winds its way alternately just west and east of north, finally swinging left by some allotments to proceed back to Bilsham Road at your starting point.

19 Halnaker SU920096 MODERATE.

Regular buses(SC) from Chichester to Boxgrove. 4 miles. R Halnaker (P), Boxgrove (S).

From the bus stop in the centre of the village of Boxgrove, begin this out-and-back journey by walking northwards up the main village street, actually called The Street, and at the crossroads at the end turn right to follow alongside the A285 through the village of Halnaker, using the pavement provided. Walk on past the end of the village, heading north-eastwards, then when the pavement gives out, continue along the roadside taking great care. Roughly half a mile from where you joined the A285, the road dips slightly and bends right, and at the bottom of the dip there's a small parking area on the left and sign for Warehead Farm; here you leave the A285 and follow the clearly signed path north-eastwards, keeping the farm buildings to your left. The path goes uphill through trees - note at one point walkers are signed away from the wider sunken path onto a narrower one to the right on slightly higher ground - and then swings decisively to the left. You emerge from the trees and now head towards Halnaker Windmill, continuing to gain height, then once on the hilltop with the windmill directly in front of you, pass through a gate with a hedge to your left. Bear left here and you will see the Halnaker trig point sitting in front of the hedge; the views are not great from the trig point itself but are very impressive from the vicinity of the windmill which you will surely want to inspect before returning the same way. Also worthy of a visit on your return journey are the Anglesey Arms, on the A285 in the centre of Halnaker, and the magnificent Boxgrove Priory Church and ruins just east of the main street and clearly signposted.

20 Slindon Folly SU955095 MODERATE.

Regular buses(SC) from Bognor Regis to Walberton. 6 miles. R Walberton (P,S), Slindon (P).

From the bus stop by the green at Walberton, follow the village street (The Street) in an easterly direction, bearing left in the village centre up Tye Lane which you follow northwards to its junction with the A27. Cross this very busy road with great care, going straight over to join Mill Road, which you follow as far as another very busy road, the A29. Again taking great care, cross this road straight over into Reynolds Lane which takes you into the village of Slindon; Reynolds Lane becomes School Hill and goes

uphill, passing the pretty pub and swinging left (westwards) along Top Road. You pass turnings to Dyers Lane and Church Hill which are to your left and the RC Church which is to your right. Just beyond the church the road veers to the right, then swings sharply left; don't swing left with the road, but go straight ahead onto a path heading downhill through the woods to reach another road. Turn right onto the road and follow it very briefly to the Courthill Farm buildings which are to your left, but just before these buildings, turn left onto a signed footpath heading north-east. You may have to negotiate cordons erected to keep cattle from straying. In a few hundred yards, you come to a large barn, marked on OS maps as Row's Barn, and here you bear right onto a signed path heading uphill; you

The Slindon Folly trig point, dwarfed by the folly itself

actually have the choice between a wide stony track or a narrower grassy path, running parallel with each other, but both take you to the remarkable flint-built Folly, the trig point immediately in front of it. The views from here are magnificent including a wide section of coastline. Return to the path junction at Row's Barn and turn right, passing the barn and going forward to another path junction in the shade of trees. Don't swing right with the main path but continue westwards on a narrower path to a further path T-junction; bear left here and walk southwards to arrive at a road, onto which you turn left. Pass a right-hand road turning but very shortly beyond this turning, turn right onto a woodland path protected by a barrier, evidently to deter motorists or bikers. Follow the attractive well-defined path, ignoring side turnings and crossing paths, reaching a car park and walking through it to arrive at Duke's Road. Turn left onto the road and head for the junction with the A27 - the roar of which will have been with you for much of the woodland walking - but just before this junction turn left onto a signed bridlepath heading east, the traffic and its noise very obvious to your right. The path kinks a little just at the very end to arrive at a T-junction with Park Lane; turn left here and follow the lane for about a quarter of a mile, then bear right onto a signed footpath which proceeds south-eastwards along the left-hand edge of woodland to arrive at the A29. Cross straight over with care onto a path which leads you almost immediately to a T-junction of paths where you turn right, then follow a bridlepath through the woods just west of south till you reach a path junction with bridleway signs pointing south and east. Proceed straight on southwards, go over a crossroads of bridlepaths and emerge from the woods to continue southwards to the A27, your last major road crossing! Again taking great care, cross straight over to join the bridlepath on the other side, and follow it, going forward into Copse Lane and proceeding past houses to arrive at West Walberton Lane. Turn left onto this road and almost immediately you will find yourself back at the start.

21 Barpham Hill/Blackpatch Hill TQ066094/096096 STRENUOUS.
Regular trains serving Arundel and Pulborough on Chichester-Horsham line; regular buses(SC) serving Storrington on Worthing-Pulborough-Midhurst route. 10.5 miles. R Arundel (P,C,S), Storrington (P,C,S).

This is a superb linear walk in classic Downland scenery starting from Arundel station. Leave the station by proceeding to the immediately adjacent A27, turning right and following it briefly south-eastwards from the station, then bear very shortly left onto the road signposted Burpham. Follow the road for a mile to Warningcamp, going over a crossroads in the village, then a couple of hundred yards beyond the crossroads, still on the road, you enter an area of trees. Bear right here onto a bridleway, joining the signed Monarch's Way, then, contouring the hillside, you walk through the woods eastwards, emerge from the woods and continue along the hillside, swinging north-east. A path comes in from the right to join yours; you continue briefly on the same path then shortly turn right, just north of east, keeping to the Monarch's Way on a dry valley bottom. Your path enters an area of trees and reaches a T-junction of paths; here you turn left and shortly reach a path crossroads, bearing right, steeply uphill through the woods. At the top of the hill you reach another path junction, at which, keeping to the Monarch's Way, you turn left onto a wide metalled track and follow it along the hilltop - don't drop back down into the valley - for about three quarters of a mile, heading just north of east. Watch for a field on the left, separating two swathes of woodland. On the far side of the field turn left onto a signed bridlepath that follows the right-hand field edge then, climbing steadily, pulls away from the woodland and heads north-eastwards for the buildings of Upper Barpham. Follow the obvious path past the farm buildings; beyond them continue north-eastwards, shortly taking a signed bridlepath going off to

Windswept but spectacular - the Blackpatch Hill trig point

the left. Keeping to an obvious track heading a little west of north, you soon reach the Barpham Hill trig point just to the left of the path, enjoying superb views down to Arundel and a large area of coastline. Follow the path on north-westwards, initially on the grassy open hilltop, then through some trees and downhill to a junction with another track; bear right onto this track and follow it eastwards past the Lee Farm buildings, going downhill beyond the buildings to reach a path junction. Here you bear right to follow a path* heading southwards along the lower slopes of Harrow Hill then swinging south-eastwards to reach a farm road.** (Note: the single-asterisked path above isn't clearly signed; you may find yourself on that farm road for the duration. This swings south-westwards then sharply south-eastwards to reach the point double-asterisked above.) At the double-asterisked point, follow a signed (yellow arrow) footpath north-eastwards away from the farm road uphill; initially signposted away from the fence to the left, it then rejoins it and you walk downhill parallel with the fence to a path sign at the edge of woodland. Bear left to enter the wood and follow a narrow hillside path northwards through the trees veering eastwards, emerging from the woods at a stile and continuing eastwards along the valley floor. Continue in the same direction on a very indistinct path which heads uphill to reach a gate and T-junction with a surprisingly faint bridlepath; turn left to follow this bridlepath which heads just north of east to a T-junction with a clearer bridlepath. You need to turn right onto this clearer path but you can conveniently cut the corner, climbing to join it and heading south-east along it. Immediately ahead you see the huge green mass which is Blackpatch Hill, the location of your second trig point; the bridlepath veers gently to the right along the lower slope of the hill, but having passed through a gate you need to head straight up to reach the top. It's a tough but fairly short climb, and the reward is a superb 360-degree view, including a long coastal strip and Chanctonbury Ring on the South Downs. You are over 500ft above the sea, having started your walk at virtually zero. Retrace your steps to the bridlepath and continue back on yourself, but this time keep going north-westwards, uphill, taking care to move away from the fence along the clear track. You reach the hilltop where you meet the South Downs Way at Chantry Post, passing to the left of the car park and joining the road heading north; as it shortly swings right, bear left onto a bridlepath heading north-west and slightly uphill. In a few hundred yards fork right onto a signed bridlepath which drops very steeply towards Storrington, clearly visible below. Ignoring a footpath going off to the right, swing left, still descending, and swing left again to arrive at the top end of a clear farm track. Join the track and head just east of north, passing Greyfriars Farm and going north into Greyfriars Lane, proceeding into the village of Storrington with an excellent range of amenities. The bus stand for buses to Pulborough station is clearly signposted.

22 Park Farm, Arundel/Arundel Park/Tortington
SU998082/TQ019092/010057 STRENUOUS.

Regular trains serving Arundel on Chichester-Horsham line. 9 miles maximum (4 for Park Farm, 3 further for Arundel Park, 2 further for Tortington). R Arundel (P,C,S). NOTE: DOGS ARE NOT PERMITTED IN ARUNDEL PARK.

From the square in the centre of Arundel make your way up the High Street, forking left into Maltravers Street and walking down to the roundabout junction of A27 and A284; bear right to cross the A284 (Dorking/Pulborough road) then before reaching the A27 Chichester road crossing, turn right onto a lane signed for the trout fishery. Almost immediately bear left at a path junction onto a signed bridleway which climbs gently through woodland, passing just to the right of Arundel Hospital. At the top (western) end of the wood you reach another path junction. Don't go straight ahead out of the wood over the stile, but turn right to continue along the bridleway through the wood beside its western fringe. Shortly a lane from the Park Farm estate comes in from the left; continue in what is a north-westerly direction past a house*, ignoring paths going off to the right and keeping the edge of the wood just to your left. In a few hundred yards, still climbing gently, you reach a gate. Don't pass through the gate but bear left onto a signed path that heads due west into open fields, leaving the wood behind. You go through a gate and continue westwards to shortly reach a clear field-edge path going to the right, just west of north. Follow this path and you will shortly see the Park Farm trig point just to your right; the views from here to the coast are magnificent, from the Isle of Wight in the west to Littlehampton and beyond looking east. You could just retrace your steps all the way back to Arundel, but for variety, when reaching the house asterisked above, you can turn hard left (a hairpin turn effectively) along a clear path steeply downhill. At the bottom turn hard right to follow a path south-eastwards that turns into a metalled track and passes the trout fishery. In due course it arrives back at the A27/A284 roundabout junction, from which you can return up Maltravers Street to access the centre of Arundel.

The Arundel Park trig point can be conveniently explored immediately following return to Arundel, or as a separate expedition. It's quite a short walk and ideal for a Sunday stroll with the bonus of a popular on-route pub! Walk down the High Street in Arundel, along the left-hand side past the post office, then bear left just before the bridge into Mill Road, passing the Norfolk Centre and proceeding along a delightful avenue with the bowls club, putting green and children's park on the right, going forward to cross the pedestrian footbridge over a channel. Go straight on along the road, then shortly pass Swanbourne Lake and, immediately beyond the lake, bear left through a gateway, keeping the lake to your left and the Swanbourne tea rooms to the right. Continue along the clear path with the lake to your left. Keep along the path beyond the end of the lake, arriving at a crossroads of paths. Ignore those going straight ahead and hard left, but take the one bearing right and now follow it as it veers northwards uphill. This is quite a slog but the views get better and better the more height you gain. During your ascent, you'll notice a large area of woodland coming in from the right; as the path on the ground gets less distinct, aim for the far left-hand side of the woods, effectively on the shoulder of the rise, and you will arrive at a gate. Pass through the gate, woodland

The Tortington trig point on a glorious July morning

now immediately to the right, and go forward to a crossroads of paths, at the very top edge of the north-east facing escarpment. Turn right to follow a clear track south-eastwards, with woodland immediately to your right and the ground falling away to the left, with magnificent views across the Arun valley; you pass an area of woodland which is to your left and arrive at an area of open pasture with another area of woodland a little way ahead of you. The path now heads south-eastwards downhill, but by looking southwards along the top of the escarpment you'll see the Arundel Park trig point ahead of you, and you'll need to leave your path to visit it. The views from the trig point are breathtaking, incorporating a large area of coastline, the Arun valley and the majestic Arundel Castle, while looking eastwards and down to the Arun valley you'll see the spire of South Stoke Church. Taking that as your line, head eastwards across the grass and you'll be reunited with your path. Turn right onto this path and now head quite steeply downhill, south-eastwards, veering in a more easterly direction to arrive at a road; join the road, keeping in the same direction, then take the first right-hand road turning (ignoring the road straight ahead signposted Offham) and descend to the popular Black Rabbit pub. From the pub you can now return to Arundel either by walking along the riverbank or the road which incidentally passes the popular Wildfowl & Wetlands Trust, well worth a visit.

For a final trig point walk based at Arundel, follow Tarrant Street, the first left turn off the town square looking up the hill, to its far end then bear left onto a walkway bringing you down to the riverside. Proceed along the riverside path and under the bridge carrying the A27 then continue along the right bank of the Arun on the riverside path downstream. Once you have left the houses of Arundel behind, now in the area known as Tortington, look out for the Tortington trig point on your right at the south end of a field below the embankment, shortly after the river has veered slightly left from just west of south to more southwards. Accessing the trig point can only be achieved by crossing a bridge and barbed wire fence giving access to the field beyond, then crossing that field in a diagonal north-westerly direction and crossing further barbed wire into the first field, heading eastwards from there back to the trig point! This is strictly private(refer to introductory notes) and signs warn you to beware of the bull, so maybe this trig point is best observed from the legitimate embankment path. Retrace your steps back to Arundel.

23 Flexham Park, near Petworth TQ011222 MODERATE.

Regular buses(SC) serving Petworth on Worthing-Pulborough-Midhurst route. 5 miles. R Petworth (P,C,S).

The walk starts outside the church in the centre of Petworth. From outside the church, cross the main road and turn right into Barton Lane which leaves the main road on a sharp corner and goes away south-eastwards, veering left(eastwards) and going forward to a gate and a path crossroads on the edge of lovely countryside. Go straight on downhill eastwards, crossing a bridge over a stream and then going uphill on an obvious path, still eastwards, keeping woodland to your left. Your path veers in a north-easterly direction, climbing gradually and enjoying beautiful views back to Petworth and to downland countryside. Follow the direction shown by the signposts, passing just to the left of one small plantation of trees and then to the right of another, aiming for a signpost in the hedge beyond the plantations, crossing a track and continuing as signed uphill, with woodland now to your right. You arrive at a junction of tracks as you enter woodland, and a sign saying you're now on Brinksole Heath. Turn right as signed and proceed south-eastwards on a clear track; ignore the signpost pointing right just before the T-junction with the road, but go forward to the road and turn left to follow it. In a few hundred yards at a left bend there's a minor road going off to the right+. Turn right to follow it for a few yards, but almost immediately turn left onto a signed bridlepath which you now follow eastwards through the woodland of Flexham Park. You drop gently downhill initially, then rise gradually, enjoying a lovely woodland walk on a clear track, ignoring crossing tracks. About three quarters of a mile from where you joined the bridleway, the track, having gained height almost throughout since the initial descent, now begins to descend. Just as it starts the descent you reach a crossroads of paths, and turn left onto the crossing track.* (If you miss it, don't worry; go forward to the road then backtrack, over one crossroads and the next is the one you want; turn right!). Follow the track which initially goes to the right then veers left. As it straightens out, but BEFORE it starts to descend, look for a tree stump just to the right of the path, and no more than 15 yards beyond it turn left into the woods, forging a gap through the trees to arrive at the trig point which is deep in the woods but easily found by following these instructions. Now you have a choice. You could just backtrack to Petworth as you arrived. Or for variety you could retrace your steps to the asterisked track crossing, turn left and descend to the road; turn right here and very shortly reach a road bend with two forked footpaths leaving the road to the right. Take the first (right-hand) of the two paths and follow it south-westwards through the woods to arrive at a road at the hamlet of Riverhill. Turn right to follow the road** for about half a mile then bear right again onto a farm track just before the woodland on the right-hand side, and immediately left onto a rather overgrown path through the woods. This arrives at the A283 by the Welldiggers Arms to the right, from which there are buses back to Petworth or the other way to Pulborough(or you can go past the pub and walk beside the A283 to Petworth - not the greatest walk!). To avoid a tedious road walk back to Petworth, you could, having joined the road double-asterisked above at Riverhill, take the first right road turn, returning you to the point marked + above. You can from here retrace your steps to Petworth - a rather pleasanter option than the A283 road walk.

24 Hesworth Common TQ005193 MODERATE.

Regular buses(SC) serving Fittleworth on Worthing-Pulborough-Midhurst route. 0.75 miles. R Fittleworth (P,S).

From the centre of Fittleworth proceed alongside the A283 south-westwards away from the village uphill to the point where the B2138 Bury/Arundel road comes up to meet it. Turn left to walk very briefly by the B2138 then turn right into a car park under the wooden entrance markers, and from here you go straight ahead along a signed path south-westwards through the woods of Hesworth Common to reach a multi-path junction. Turn right here and go steeply uphill just west of north to reach the trig point from which the views to the South Downs are quite fantastic - great reward for such modest effort! Continue along the path, now losing height quickly, turning first right then first right again to return to the car park, then retrace your steps to Fittleworth.

The Hesworth Common trig point with a fine downland backdrop

25 Greatham TQ038156 MODERATE.

Regular trains serving Pulborough and Amberley on Chichester-Horsham line. 6 miles. R Pulborough (P,C,S), Amberley (P), Houghton Bridge (P,C).

This walk incorporates a section of delightful riverside walking and the very pretty village of Amberley. From the station at Pulborough, walk down to the main road and

The Greatham trig point in a wintry quagmire

bear left to follow it eastwards and straight over the roundabout into the village centre. Opposite the old post office, turn right down a path that descends to the river then bear left to walk along the bank. Keep along the bank till you reach a footpath sign pointing to the left, away from the river, the bank ahead blocked by a no entry sign. Follow the signed path across the meadows to a gate then continue as signposted, bearing slightly right and proceeding in a straight line across the next field, dipping gently downhill. Then, again as indicated by the signpost, turn left and proceed to a gate leading to a track that goes quite steeply uphill to the beautiful little church at Wiggonholt which dates back as far as the 13th century. Proceed to the small car park area and church signboard, adjacent to which you climb over a stile and follow the footpath leading southwards from it. The path initially descends, then gently climbs to reach the car park of the visitor centre for the popular Pulborough Brooks nature reserve. Immediately beyond the car park the footpath arrives at a T-junction of paths; turn right here, keeping the car park and visitor centre to your right, and having enjoyed the fine view descend through the thick woodland. Shortly you reach another T-junction of paths, and keeping a fence immediately to your right, turn right and continue through the woods. You ascend gently, and the path swings to the left to arrive at the road linking the A283 with Coldwaltham. Turn right onto the road and follow it, passing the delightful hamlet of Greatham with its tiny 12th century church and manor house with 17th century features. Emerging from Greatham, you arrive at another row of cottages which are to your right with a very conspicuous phone box opposite, beyond which you'll see a field rising to your left. By entering this field and climbing, heading fractionally west of south, you'll reach the Greatham trig point with super views southwards to the downs and north to the Arun valley. However there is no public right of way across the field, accessed only by climbing over a choice of gates either side of the phone box, and you should refer to my introductory notes. Retrace your steps to the road and continue westwards along it, at length reaching the Greatham Bridge crossing of the Arun. Just before the bridge you turn left onto a signed path, initially following the riverbank, then leaving the riverside and ascending gently along the path to reach a T-junction with a sandy track. Turn right onto this track and follow it past a house and chicken run, just past which you bear sharp left, keeping a high hedge on your left-hand side. Proceed along the track, following the signposting which directs you sharply right and downhill, then bear sharp left just beyond the house at the foot of the hill; shortly turn right again immediately beyond a fence into an area of lush grass punctuated by marsh plants. The path, which is here rather indistinct on the ground, doesn't proceed exactly parallel with the fence but goes at a slight angle to it, aiming for a footbridge. The surroundings hereabouts are absolutely delightful; although you are some way from the Arun itself, you are now back in the Arun valley with constantly improving views to the majestic South Downs escarpment. Cross the footbridge and continue, heading in a virtually straight line for Amberley, until you reach a T-junction with a wider track. Turn right at this junction and follow the track which in a few hundred yards leaves the valley floor and climbs briefly to a T-junction with a road. When you arrive at the road, turn right and go forward to the junction with Amberley's main street. Turn right onto this street, a delightful mixture of thatch, tile, timber, flint, brick and stone, and follow it past the village pottery and Norman church. Close by is Amberley Castle, a square-towered construction dating back to the 1370's to defend the upper reaches of the Arun valley. The road peters out and becomes a public footpath, initially metalled but continuing as a dirt track; keep on the track to the railway, crossing with great care, then carry on as signposted across the fields. At length you arrive at the river bank, then turn left to follow it as far as the B2139 at Houghton Bridge. Turn left to follow the road, passing the tempting tea gardens, and pass under the railway bridge, turning right immediately beyond it to reach Amberley Station.

26 Brookfield Park, Toddington TQ047034 EASY.

Regular buses(SC) serving start/finish point on Worthing-Littlehampton route. 0.75 miles. R none.

This walk starts at the roundabout junction of Worthing Road(Rustington) and Windsor Drive at Toddington between Rustington and Littlehampton. From the roundabout, head briefly westwards towards Littlehampton along Worthing Road, on the right-hand (north) side. Very soon a blue signed cycleway/pedestrian way starts on the right; go forward to join this, but almost immediately - and just before the brown LITTLEHAMPTON town sign - turn right up a footpath/cyclepath indicated by a wooden Brookfield Park post. Follow this path for a couple of hundred yards, looking out for a concrete car park immediately bordering the path on your left. Go briefly forward from there, with terraced housing to your left and a fence to your right with a wooded gully behind the fence; look carefully to your right and, in a small gap, shortly beyond the car park referred to above, you will see the trig point immediately behind the fence. The views are pretty much non-existent, although looking up the cycle path there's a tantalising glimpse of some higher ground on the horizon on a clear day! From here you could just retrace your steps to the start but if you wanted a longer and more rewarding walk you could follow the cycle path to its end and then bear left into the attractive Brookfield Park open space, a pleasant amenity with a lake and play area for children. You'll then need to retrace your steps to Worthing Road from there.

Robust wooden protection for the Brookfield Park, Toddington trig point

Trig point exploring leads you to many beautiful and historic landmarks in Sussex. This is the very attractive Knepp Castle estate with its elegant Norman castle, to be found on West Sussex walk 33.

West Sussex Walks 27 - 40
South Downs Way section starts 4 - 6

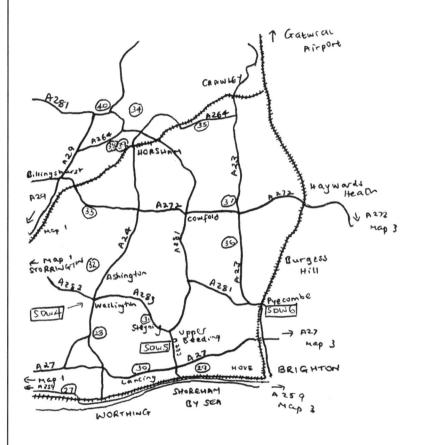

27 Highdown Hill TQ093043 MODERATE.

Regular trains serving Goring-by-Sea on Portsmouth-Brighton line. 3 miles. R Highdown (P,C).

This is an ideal Sunday afternoon walk. From the north side of Goring-by-Sea station walk up the approach road, Goring Street, to a junction with the A259 and bear left to follow a footpath/cycle path to a roundabout. Turn left at the roundabout and walk beside the A259 for about a quarter of a mile using the pedestrian way provided, then cross the road with great care and walk up a road signposted Highdown Gardens heading just west of north away from the A259; the road ends at a car park close by the entrance to the gardens, which are free to enter and well worth a visit. Exit the top side of the car park and bear left onto an obvious path uphill, although there's no obligation to stick to the path. Keep climbing, and soon you will be enjoying tremendous views to the sea and to Worthing; at the top of the hill you can clearly identify the old hillfort to the right, and by climbing to the fort itself you will see the Highdown Hill trig point from which the views are magnificent, with the tops of the South Downs clearly visible to the north. You could just retrace your steps to the car park and gardens - there's a good

The Highdown Hill trig point on a sunlit Boxing Day morning

restaurant and tea room to the left of the entrance to the gardens - or you could follow a lovely green path westwards to an old windmill, beautifully situated on the hillside but now bereft of sails. On your way to the windmill you'll notice a footpath sign pointing left - downhill - and the signed path takes you down to the A259 again. You could then turn left to follow the A259 eastwards back to the roundabout mentioned above. However you may prefer to retrace your steps to the car park and gardens; there are so many different path options and the scenery from the hillside is so diverse that it won't feel like "going back the same way!"

28 Cissbury Ring TQ141082 STRENUOUS.

Regular buses(SC) serving Findon Road(A24)/May Tree Avenue junction and Findon on Worthing-Pulborough-Midhurst route. 3 miles. R Findon(P,S).

The walk actually starts at the Storrington Rise car park; to access it from the bus stop at the Findon Road(A24)/May Tree Avenue junction, walk briefly eastwards up May Tree Avenue, then as May Tree Avenue swings sharply right, continue just north of east up Storrington Rise to arrive at a sharp right bend. Don't swing right into Long Meadow but bear left into the Storrington Rise car park. Bear left into the field adjacent to the left side of the car park and walk to the top left corner of that field to join a signed bridleway heading north-eastwards, uphill. It's quite a narrow path at first, keeping woodland to the left, then widens and swings left to pass through the middle of woodland, gaining height all the time. You emerge from woodland, passing through a gate, and now enjoy a splendid open climb with fine views to Findon village to the left. Keep climbing to reach a gate which you pass through, then continue along a green track to reach another gate* just the other side of which is a car parking area; don't go through the gate but turn hard right along a wide green track, soon reaching a crossing track. Don't turn right or left onto this track but go straight over onto a stepped path which bends first right, then left, climbing steeply. You pass over another crossing track

The trig point at Cissbury Ring, an immensely popular viewpoint

and continue up steps to reach the Cissbury Ring summit area; continuing in the same direction, make your way up to the highest ground to reach the Cissbury Ring trig point. The views, as you might expect, are excellent, but don't expect to be on your own, as this is a very popular area indeed. Retrace your steps to the gate asterisked above, pass through the gate and now bear left, going forward to a metalled road which you follow downhill, enjoying splendid views as you do so; at the T-junction at the bottom of the hill, bear right into Nepcote Lane and descend into the centre of Findon, which boasts an impressive range of amenities as well as bus connections.

29 Southwick Hill/Mill Hill TQ234078/212078 STRENUOUS.

Regular buses(BH) serving Mile Oak from central Brighton; regular trains serving Shoreham on Portsmouth-Brighton line. 4 miles. R Mile Oak (P,S), Shoreham (P,C,S).

From the Mile Oak pub on Mile Oak Road, Mile Oak, just north-west of Portslade, turn left and walk very briefly north-westwards up Mile Oak Road, turning almost immediately left into Oakdene Crescent. The crescent soon bends sharply right, with Oakdene Close going off to the left; just beyond the bend, look out for and walk up a narrow concrete path going off Oakdene Crescent to the left. Go forward to steps and a gate leading to open downland, continuing uphill in exactly the same direction and walking very steeply to reach another gate. Go through the gate and immediately beyond the gate turn right onto a clear path which you follow, soon reaching a fork. Here you take the right fork into an area of trees and bushes; soon you are reassured by a bridleway sign and you now follow the bridleway as signed (in fact the Monarch's Way) which proceeds north-westwards, gradually gaining height, keeping a fence to the right. Although the OS map shows this to be a wooded area it is more grassland populated by trees and bushes. You pass through a gate and continue to the top of the rise, reaching the Southwick Hill trig point which is to your left immediately adjacent to the path. Unfortunately the views are partially obscured by the bushes but you can see beyond to Shoreham and the coast. Return to the path and go forward to a gate; DON'T go through the gate but turn left for a few yards to reach another gate, turning right here to follow an undulating path westwards, with lovely views to the coastline between Shoreham and Hove. You drop down to the large Mossy Bottom Barn, beyond which you veer right as signposted up a metalled track. The track becomes rougher again but maintains an obvious course past the attractive buildings of New Erringham Farm, bends sharply left and climbs to reach a road. Turn left onto the road and follow it, looking carefully at the hilltop field to your right in the middle of which you'll see the Mill Hill trig point. There's no right of access and if you want to get to it you'll need to creep under or through the barbed wire fence (please refer to my introductory notes).

Ironically the views aren't the best from the trig point; better ones are enjoyed by returning to the road and walking past the woods that are to the right as far as the car park. From the car park there's a grandstand view of the sea, the coastline all the way from Brighton to Worthing and beyond, the Adur valley and the magnificent Lancing College Chapel. There's now an unavoidable road walk all the way on down the road, named Mill Hill. Pass over the A27 bridge and continue downhill to a T-junction; turn left into Erringham Road and follow the road south-eastwards, going forward across Upper Shoreham Road into Mill Lane. Continue to the T-junction with Buckingham Road and turn right to arrive shortly at Shoreham station and the adjacent level crossing, immediately beyond which is the town centre of Shoreham.

The Southwick Hill trig point, views from which are obscured by thick vegetation

30 Steep Down TQ168075 MODERATE, STRENUOUS IN PLACES.
Regular buses(SC) between Worthing station and Lyons Farm retail park on the A27 between Worthing and Lancing. 7 miles maximum, 5 miles minimum. R Lyons Farm (P,C,S), Shoreham (P,C,S).

This walk works well either as a straightforward journey from the start at Lyons Farm retail park to Steep Down and back - there being ample refreshment opportunity in, or at a pub/restaurant adjacent to, the retail park - or as a linear walk incorporating some delightful downland and riverside walking. The first part of this walk is undoubtedly unattractive, as you walk eastwards beside the A27 dual carriageway from the retail park for just over half a mile; much to your relief, no doubt, you leave the A27 by taking the second turning on the left, Church Lane, almost immediately passing the very conspicuous and very interesting church of St Mary, Sompting. It boasts England's finest Saxon steeple, built early in the 11th century, and inside there's some splendid Saxon sculpture and carving. Continue along Church Lane, initially north then swinging north-east, the road now marked on maps as Titch Hill, and then veer north-westwards along Titch Hill to Titch Hill Farm. At the farm buildings turn hard right, south-eastwards, along a track which soon brings you to a T-junction with another track, Dankton Lane. Turn left at the T-junction and follow it northwards, climbing steadily and keeping a line of pylons immediately to your left. You swing slightly east of north, still gaining height, to arrive at a T-junction of paths, and here you turn right to follow a clear track eastwards. Shortly this track swings to the right. Very shortly after it does so, a few yards past a gate* to the left with a path heading east beyond it, turn hard right onto a path that goes steeply uphill to arrive at the Steep Down trig point. The views are breathtaking; on a clear day you can see Bognor Regis to the west, and the cliffs beyond Brighton to the east, with excellent views also to the Adur valley, the South Downs and the Weald. Retrace your steps to the gate asterisked above from which you could now just retrace your steps to Lyons Farm. However, to create a fine linear walk, go through the gate onto the path which heads east, then veers just north of east before swinging just south of east; it's lovely walking on a good path with a reassuring fence to your right and increasingly good views ahead. You descend very gently, enjoying lovely views ahead to the Adur valley, but much closer at hand is the tiny community of Coombes, a group of houses and farm buildings that are separated from your hillside by an area of woodland. Continue alongside the fence till you get level with the wood. As you do so you approach a double gate, but immediately before this is a gate in the fence to your right; pass through the gate and continue in the same direction you've previously been following, then almost immediately on the left you'll see a signed footpath leading steeply down into the trees. Turning hard left you follow this path downhill and emerge into a field then go forward onto a metalled drive, just to the left of which is the lovely little village church of Coombes, its chief treasure being the 12th century wall paintings of the Lewes Cluniac School. Follow the drive to a T-junction and turn right into Coombes Road, then walk along Coombes Road which goes south-eastwards, veers southwards and then swings south-eastwards again to reach a little inlet channel of the river Adur. Here you join a path along the right side of the channel which goes forward to follow the right bank of the Adur. Continue along the riverside path under the Shoreham Flyover and walk on to the footbridge about a quarter of a mile beyond the flyover; cross the footbridge then bear right to follow the riverside path all the way down to Shoreham. There are regular buses and trains from Shoreham back to Worthing.

31 Steyning TQ185136 EASY.

Regular buses(BH) serving Steyning from Brighton; regular buses (SC Mon-Sat, CB Sun) serving Henfield on Horsham-Brighton route. 6 miles maximum, 4 miles minimum. R Steyning (P,C,S).

Walk from the centre of Steyning south-eastwards along the High Street, passing the Church Street junction, going downhill and turning left into Jarvis Lane. Follow this road uphill and over the A283 bypass, the road continuing just north of east and becoming King's Barn Lane, being joined by the Downs Link. The lane swings northwards, then north-westwards and then north-eastwards, going over a tributary of the river Adur and the old Shoreham-Christ's Hospital railway, and passing a sewage works. Now a track, the lane passes an isolated house and the buildings of Wyckham Dale Farm, then swings more sharply eastwards and drops down to a little valley to arrive at Wyckham Farm. You keep to the lane, swinging left to pass the farm buildings and climbing up to a footpath junction*, the Downs Link going off to the right, just south of east here. However you continue northwards along the lane, kinking right then left to pass the edge of a small area of woodland. Continue westwards, then veer right(north-westwards), losing height a little. As you swing right you will be aware of a field on the right-hand side; use a gateway to enter the field and aim for trees planted around the boundary fence along the north side of the field. The trig point is in these trees, hardly enjoying the most spectacular trig point setting! Now backtrack to the footpath junction asterisked above. You could just retrace your steps to Steyning but a more interesting option is to follow the signed Downs Link just south of east, shortly joining the course of the old Shoreham-Christ's Hospital railway. It's now a delightful walk north-eastwards, swinging just west of north, along the course of the old line through the Adur valley, crossing the river Adur and enjoying fine views back to the Downs. Just over 2 miles after joining the Downs Link, you arrive in the outskirts of Henfield; staying on the Downs Link, you leave the course of the railway to follow Station Road and reach a T-junction with Upper Station Road. Turn right into this road and follow it into the centre of the pretty village of Henfield with regular buses back to Steyning and Brighton.

31A Wolstonbury Hill TQ283138

This trig point is more conveniently explored in a linear walk incorporating two other trig points which lie outside West Sussex. Please refer to walk 2 in the East Sussex and Brighton & Hove section of this book.

32 Thakeham TQ107177 EASY.
Regular but infrequent buses(CB) serving Thakeham on Horsham-Ashington route, buses stopping at the Thakeham turning off B2139 between Storrington and Coolham. 3 miles maximum, 0.5 miles minimum. R Thakeham (P).

If you just wish to visit the trig point, walk down from the bus stop along the minor road towards Thakeham, shortly bearing left onto a signed path* leading up stone steps and then north-east along the right-hand edge of a sports field. At the top end of the field bear right down steps to continue north-east on a clear path but very soon reach a crossroads of paths and bear left (north-westwards) along a left-hand field edge on a signed path. Continue to the field corner** then swing right, continuing along the left-hand field edge to reach the trig point from which there are excellent views, particularly to Wealden countryside to the north. Return to the field corner double-asterisked above then bear right to follow the signed path into the next field, bearing left as signed over a stile into an adjacent field, crossing one further stile and descending steps to reach the road. Bear left onto the road to reach the bus stop again. If this walk seems a little tame it can be extended by continuing downhill along the road beyond the single-asterisked point, entering Thakeham and passing the White Lion pub and a left turn to the very pretty hillside church. Carry straight on beyond this turn, the road becoming a track. Go over one crossroads of paths then as the track bends right towards Thakeham Place Farm, bear left onto a signed path that heads gently uphill to arrive at the very pretty church of Warminghurst, no longer used for regular worship but beautifully kept. Return the same way, leaving the road at the single-asterisked point in order to visit the trig point as directed above.

The Thakeham trig point on a raw February afternoon

33 Coolham/Dial Post TQ114231/TQ153180 MODERATE.

Regular trains serving Billingshurst on Chichester-Horsham line; regular but infrequent buses(CB) to Horsham from Coolham on Horsham-Ashington route; regular but infrequent buses(MB Mon-Sat, CB Sun) from Knepp and A24/A272 junction on Worthing-Horsham route; regular buses(SC Mon-Sat, CB Sun) serving Partridge Green on Horsham-Brighton route. 9 miles. R Billingshurst (P,C,S), Coolham (P), Dial Post (P).

Starting from Billingshurst station, head just west of south along the road passing the station, namely Lower Station Road, effectively away from the village. Follow the road which veers south-eastwards; in just over half a mile you bear left onto a metalled signed footpath signposted South House Farm, and walk along this metalled lane, ignoring a signed path shortly veering left. In a few hundred yards the metalled lane swings sharp right, but you continue in the same south-easterly direction along a clear very straight signed path through what is most attractive open countryside. At a field boundary a signpost directs you hard left, and then shortly right to arrive at a metalled road. Turn right onto this road, shortly reaching Coneyhurst Farm, then just past the farm use a stile to turn left onto a signed grassy footpath. You follow this path, passing a magnificent farmhouse and pond, and continue beyond the farm buildings on what is a clearly defined path. This kinks right and left - at this kink, watch for a Quaker burial ground that's been used as such, as a sign says, since 1660. Beyond the burial ground continue along an enclosed path to reach another road; bear left onto this road and almost at once arrive at a T-junction with the A272, bearing right to follow beside this very busy road, fortunately with pavement provided. In about half a mile look out for a signed bridlepath on the right leading to Patman's Farm, and follow this for a few yards to reach the Coolham trig point, standing rather self-consciously on the verge. Return to the A272 and carry on south-eastwards to reach Coolham. As you walk, look across to the pleasant redbrick Albert Cottage with a very distinctive plaque on the front dedicated to Prince Albert. Coolham contains two features of note - a welcoming pub, the Selsey Arms, and an unusual war memorial which is partially written in Polish, as it commemorates a number of soldiers including Poles who were based at the nearby Coolham Advance Landing Ground Airfield which opened in 1944. If you decide to stop your walk here, the bus stop is just beside the memorial. If you're carrying on, then at the crossroads in the village, turn right - southwards - onto the B2139 and follow it briefly. Very soon, however, turn left onto a signed bridleway which goes across the site of the airfield, initially eastwards and parallel with the A272, the traffic noise clearly audible. You pass close to the pond of St Julians, effectively the source of the river Adur which is one of the most important rivers in Sussex. With the broad expanse of field that was once the airfield to the right, your track veers gently to the right then left, now heading south-eastwards and passing just to the right of a small patch of woodland. As you walk along the track, note the line of beautifully maintained memorials alongside it on your right. Soon you reach a signed bridleway junction; don't turn right here but continue in the same direction, keeping the attractive Knights Farm buildings to your left, and arriving at a road. Go straight over the road onto the signed bridleway, soon reaching a path junction; here veer left, following the signed bridleway and going down to a footbridge over the infant Adur. Beyond the bridge, veer right and climb up on a clear path through a field to a T-junction with a road; turn right onto the road and immediately enter the village of Shipley. Shipley's outstanding feature is its windmill, which is clearly visible on the right shortly after you join the road. Built in 1879 and also known as King's Mill, it is arguably the most impressive windmill in Sussex. Continue along the road until it bends left; just before the bend, turn right onto a signed path which initially follows a road then passes just to the right of the 12th century church. Beyond the church, walk on down towards the river, enjoying a lovely view of the windmill across the meadow to the right. Bear gently left to walk parallel with the left bank of the river through the meadow, soon reaching a footbridge crossing of the river. Go over the footbridge then walk past the left side of Church Farm South, going forward to a lane and following it to a T-junction with a metalled road; turn left onto the road, following it and soon arriving at a road junction, continuing in the same direction, just south of east. You pass two signed footpath turnings off to the left, keeping to the road and going over a bridge crossing a wide tributary of the Adur. Still following the road, you begin to rise until in a few hundred yards you reach another signed footpath going off to the left*. To get to the second trig point, you need to do a "spur" walk here but if you're pushed for time you could leave it out and resume the walk at the point double-asterisked below. The spur walk is as follows. Continue along the road to the village of Dial Post, turning right at the T-junction and following the road to reach and cross the A24(take great care). Joining the Ashurst road on the other side, follow it for half a mile or so to a point where footpaths meet the road from both right and left; take the footpath going right which heads

Winter shadows on and beside the roadside trig point at Coolham

through woodland then emerges shortly into a field. Climb to the top of the field to reach the Dial Post trig point, with excellent views to the Downs especially Chanctonbury Ring. Retrace your steps to the road, going straight over onto a signed path that heads south-eastwards, then soon swings left and comes to a footpath crossroads. Bear left here to follow a path through the woods, heading first just west of north then just east of north - it's a nice wide clear path but could be spongy after wet weather. Emerge from the woods and go forward through a field to Thistleworth Farm, taking a driveway round the left side of the farm buildings; beyond the buildings, turn left as signed up a steep bank, then drop down the other side of the bank again as signed and go forward to a stile giving access to a road crossing of the A24. Having crossed with extreme care, follow the signed path as shown north-eastwards through fields, negotiating a couple of electric fences to arrive at a road. Bear left onto the road to arrive back in Dial Post, then turn shortly right along Swallows Lane to make your way back to the path turning single-asterisked above. **Follow it as signed just north of east, with fine views to Knepp Castle across the fields to your right; the path isn't terribly clear through the field, but aim for an attractive house on the other side of the little Adur valley and drop down to cross a footbridge over the Adur. The path is much clearer on the other side of the bridge, and you follow it north-east to reach a T-junction with the Knepp Castle estate road. Turn right onto the road, shortly passing Knepp Castle which is to your right. Built by William de Braose soon after the Norman invasion, it was used as a hunting lodge but was allowed to fall into ruin and during the 18th century nearly all the remaining stone was used to build a road. Walk on along the estate road to reach a junction with the A24 and turn left, soon reaching a bus stop from which there are regular but not hugely frequent buses to Horsham with train connections from there back to Billingshurst. If your wait for the bus is going to be excessive, you might consider crossing the A24 (with immense care), turning left and then shortly bearing right onto the B2135 which in 3 miles brings you to Partridge Green where you'll find a pub, shops and hourly buses back to Horsham. Or you could walk northwards along the left side of the A24 for just over half a mile to the junction with the A272 where there's a supermarket and McDonalds. Here you can enjoy a coffee before making your way to the bus stop with shelter by the A24 on the far side of the A272 crossing.

34 Warnham TQ156343 EASY.
Regular buses(A) serving Warnham on Horsham-Dorking route. 1 mile. R Warnham (P,S).

From the junction of School Hill and Bell Road in the centre of the village of Warnham, walk down to the very impressive village church, cross the road and follow the signed metalled footpath westwards past the Sussex Oak pub and then forward past the village

The ivyclad Warnham trig point

primary school, soon arriving at the junction of Lucas Road and Freeman Road. Bear left into Lucas Road and follow it westwards to a T-junction with Tilletts Lane; turn right up Tilletts Lane and follow it uphill, then take the first right turn into Threestile Road. Shortly on your left you reach a turning to Cider Mill Farm, and by bearing left onto the farm approach road you'll find the trig point just before the entrance gate on the left. The views are best to the north-east and there are also good views southwards from the other side of Threestile Road. Return to Threestile Road and follow it south-eastwards downhill, soon reaching the large village green which is on your right, and which you can cut across to return to the attractive village centre.

35 Colgate TQ227330 EASY.

Regular but infrequent buses(MB) serving Colgate and Faygate on Horsham-Crawley route. 0.5 miles. R Colgate (P).

Looking outwards from the bus shelter at Colgate, beside the pub, turn right and then immediately left up Tower Road which you follow for just over a quarter of a mile, keeping forestry on both sides. You then reach a track going off to the right (if you come to a water tower on the left you've gone too far); half-hidden in the bushes immediately to the right of this track turning is a round "pepperpot" construction with a graffiti inscription ("B Baker 1943 Vancouver") but please note this isn't the trig point itself! To access the trig point, retrace your steps for a few yards back along the road beside a wall, then as soon as the wall stops turn left and proceed through the trees to reach the trig point, lying no more than 30 or 40 yards from the road. There's no path to speak of, but by walking in a straight line from the road you'll get there without too much difficulty. From the trig point, nestling in trees with no views, return to the road; you could return to Colgate for a drink at the pub before the next bus, or continue on the road to Faygate from where buses are more frequent.

36 Twineham TQ254205 EASY.

Regular buses(MB) serving Hickstead on Brighton-Crawley route. 3 miles. R Hickstead (P).

To begin this walk, head westwards away from Hickstead village and A23 crossing along Hickstead Lane, arriving at a T-junction with Bolney Chapel Road; turn right along this road and follow it over the river, soon reaching the Bob Lane turning to the left

The South Downs Way escarpment is just visible in this view of the Twineham trig point

which you follow, soon descending and bending sharply left. Just before the road bends right, look out for a gate on the left which was locked at the time of writing. Assuming you have permission or are prepared to take the risk - please refer to my introductory notes - turn left over or under the gate and head north-eastwards along the left-hand field edge with the hedge to your left, rising to reach the trig point. The views to the South Downs escarpment are very attractive. You could either retrace your steps from here or continue beyond the trig point in the same direction to the field boundary beyond, negotiate the barbed wire fence, and cross the field beyond diagonally to a gate beside the junction of Bob Lane and Bolney Chapel Road, surmounting the gate and retracing your steps from there. Just before reaching the junction with Hickstead Lane you could bear right onto a signed path consisting of a green strip across a field taking you to Twineham School, immediately beyond which is the attractive St Peter's Church. From the path leading to the school there's a good view of the trig point and the very splendid house just behind it. You can now retrace your steps along the path or, having reached the school, turn left onto a road that leads to a T-junction; turn left here to arrive back at the junction of Bolney Chapel Road and Hickstead Lane, and head back to Hickstead the way you came.

37 Bolney TQ257249 EASY.

Regular buses(MB) serving Bolney on Brighton-Crawley route. 3 miles. R Bolney (P).

From the pub in Bolney walk northwards up Bolney Street, continuing straight up the hill beyond the crossroads of Bolney Lodge Lane and Cherry Lane. The road peters out and becomes a path which you continue to follow just west of north through Wykehurst Park, crossing various stiles with High Weald Landscape Trail waymarks - the path is very clearly defined in attractive mostly wooded countryside. You drop down to a stream then climb, passing a profusion of gorse and bluebells, to reach Jeremy's Lane, turning left to follow it to a T-junction where you turn right into Colwood Lane. Just beyond the houses on the right there's a field with a gate in the near corner; to reach the trig point you'll need to go over the gate into what is private land - you should refer to my introductory notes - then walk for a few yards, and you'll see the trig point nestling in the hedge on the right. From the trig point retrace your steps to the junction of Colwood Lane and Jeremy's Lane. To return to Bolney you can go back the same way, or for variety (but more road walking) when you reach the junction with Jeremy's Lane walk on down Colwood Lane, then at the T-junction turn left into Cross Colwood Lane; follow this past the Bolney Lodge Lane turning, shortly beyond which you turn left along a footpath which brings you back to Bolney Street.

38 Sharpenhurst Hill, near Itchingfield TQ138282 EASY.

Regular trains serving Christ's Hospital on Chichester-Horsham line. 2 miles. R none.

Walk from the main forecourt of Christ's Hospital station(down platform) along Station Road, turning right at the end into King Edward Road and then bearing right onto Christ's Hospital Road, crossing the railway. Follow Christ's Hospital Road to the T-junction with Westons Hill and turn left onto this road. Go gently uphill, past the right turn to Itchingfield, then very shortly turn left onto a signed footpath. This keeps woodland immediately to the left initially; you then leave the woodland behind and continue on an obvious path across pasture, climbing gently onto what is Sharpenhurst Hill. You then reach another footpath sign - the hilltop, decorated with bushes and a mast, a little way to the right - and here you in fact take the path which makes for the mast. As you arrive at the bushes you'll see the trig point from which there are lovely views to the impressive buildings of Christ's Hospital, the town of Horsham, and also Itchingfield Church just to the north-west. Return to the main path and turn right to continue along it, going downhill and passing through an area of woodland which is dotted with bluebells in spring. Exit the woodland and go forward to descend an embankment to cross the railway line, taking great care; you climb up the embankment the other side, and drop down another embankment to reach the old Shoreham-Christ's Hospital line. Turn left to follow the old line, now on the Downs Link footpath, and just follow the Downs Link north-eastwards as signed, parallel with the extant railway, passing just to the left of the grounds and buildings of Christ's Hospital School and arriving at the junction of King Edward Road and Christ's Hospital Road. Retrace your steps via King Edward Road and Station Road to return to the station.

39 The Haven/Baynards TQ089309/078345 MODERATE.

Regular trains serving Christ's Hospital on Chichester-Horsham line; regular buses(A) serving Rudgwick on Horsham-Cranleigh/Guildford route. 9 miles maximum, 7 miles minimum. R Rudgwick (P,S).

This walk can be done either as a linear walk starting from Christ's Hospital or as an "out and back" walk from Rudgwick. The linear walk, which is to be preferred, is as follows. From Christ's Hospital station follow the directions for walk 38 (Sharpenhurst Hill) above, as far as the T-junction of Christ's Hospital Road and Westons Hill. However this time you turn right and follow Westons Hill just east of north past Weston's Farm. Shortly beyond the farm the road bends sharp left; turn right here onto a narrow road, crossing a bridge over the old Christ's Hospital to Guildford railway. Just beyond the bridge turn left along a signed Downs Link path that proceeds onto the course of the old railway and provides lovely easy walking. In a mile and a half you pass the housing and industrial development just south of Slinfold and shortly beyond that you cross the very busy A29. A few hundred yards beyond that, still on the old railway, you reach an overbridge* with BRIGHTON WALKERS chalked on the brickwork; immediately before the bridge, turn right up the steps then hard left across the bridge and through a gate on a tarmac path. This proceeds south-westwards uphill, then swings sharply right and continues past the buildings of Kilsyth with a golf course to the left. As the tarmac track swings right, bear left as signposted to continue beside the golf course but this time along the grass, heading in roughly the same direction; soon you bear right along the signed path away from the golf course, entering the woods. You go over a stile in fencing and steeply downhill to cross a bridge over a stream, then continue straight up the other side, although at the time of writing the footpath sign here misleadingly pointed a route parallel with the stream. Having climbed up from the bridge, the path levels out, but take care to bear left as signposted shortly; in spring this woodland is particularly beautiful with its profusion of bluebells and primroses. The path is clear and leads you to the west end of the wood. Keeping a gully and trees to your left, just follow the left-hand field edge as signposted, crossing a number of stiles, to arrive at Haven Road. Turn right and very shortly left into a field just past the sign

The Baynards trig point, right on the border of Surrey and Sussex

for Havenhurst to meet The Haven trig point from which there are fine views westwards. Now retrace your steps all the way back to the overbridge asterisked above, and rejoin the Downs Link old railway walk. This brings you, in 2 miles, to the village of Rudgwick where you can pick up a bus to Horsham and then a train back to Christ's Hospital. If you wished to explore a trig point which is right on the border between West Sussex and Surrey (in fact just into Surrey) you could continue along the Downs Link old railway walk for just under a mile beyond Rudgwick to its meeting with the Sussex Border Path. Turn left to follow the Sussex Border Path, clearly signed, through woodland; it shares its route initially with the Downs Link bridleway but this route goes off to the right and you carry on briefly westwards along the Sussex Border Path. Just before the path emerges from the wood you bear right onto a woodland path which takes you to the "border" trig point a little south of the hamlet at Baynards. It has an attractive woodland setting which is especially pretty if there are bluebells about. Now retrace your steps to Rudgwick. The "out and back" walk is as follows. From the centre of Rudgwick, make your way to the Downs Link old railway path which is easily accessible from the village centre via the Medical Centre car park. Assuming you choose to visit the "border" trig point first, turn right onto the Downs Link and follow the description as set out for the linear walk above. Then having visited the Baynards trig point and retraced your steps, continue south-east on the Downs Link and immediately beyond the asterisked overbridge above, turn left up the steps and follow the directions to The Haven trig point again as set out in the linear description above. You could then choose to go back to Rudgwick the same way, or (for a shorter but less attractive circular walk) continue north-westwards for just under 2 miles along Haven Road to reach the A281 at Bucks Green. Turn right and then shortly left to arrive back in the centre of Rudgwick.

40 Rowhook TQ122339 EASY.

Regular buses(A) on Horsham-Slinfold-Rudgwick-Cranleigh/Guildford route(see route description below). 4 miles maximum, 1 mile minimum. R Rowhook (P).

The easiest way to undertake this walk using public transport is to ask the bus driver on the journey either from Rudgwick or from Horsham to drop you off at the roundabout junction of the A29 and A281 a mile or so north of Slinfold. Head eastwards for just a few yards along the A281 from the roundabout but almost immediately bear left onto a signed public bridleway heading just east of north uphill through the woods; despite the wooded surroundings there are good views through the trees on the right. Keep uphill along the path which eventually levels out and passes through a garden, becoming metalled and reaching a T-junction with a metalled drive. Turn right here and almost at once reach another T-junction; by turning left you would soon (and may wish to

The house in the woods - a pleasant backdrop to the Rowhook trig point

anyway!) reach the pretty pub at Rowhook, but you need to turn right (signed Waterland) and then straight away left into a field where you will see the trig point ahead of you. To get back to civilisation you could retrace your steps and hope the driver of the next bus will see you (a rather risky strategy), or failing that you could walk south-westwards down the A281 to the next bus stop or left at the next road junction (a mile from the roundabout) to reach Slinfold where there are amenities as well as buses. Or you could walk to Rowhook, turn left onto the road and in just under a mile turn left to follow the signed Sussex Border Path for just under 2 miles back into the centre of Rudgwick.

41 Plaistow/Loxwood TQ000309/043302 EASY.

VERY LIMITED buses(A) serving Plaistow and Loxwood from Guildford, Godalming and Cranleigh; VERY LIMITED buses(CB) serving Plaistow and Loxwood from Horsham. 5.5 miles maximum, 3 miles minimum. R Plaistow (P), Loxwood (P,S).

Please note that at the time of writing the Arriva bus link to Plaistow had been suspended but there were regular buses to Loxwood from Godalming and Guildford. If

The Plaistow trig point has clearly seen better days

the service to Plaistow hasn't been reinstated when you read this, you'll need to start from Loxwood and do the walk to Plaistow as described below in reverse then return the way you came. From the centre of Plaistow, follow the main village street (The Street) north past the church then swing immediately left to follow the road just south of west past the Nell Ball housing estate. As the road swings right, turn left (south) onto a signed footpath, then just before the first field boundary on the right bear right, over the low wire fence, and go steeply uphill (westwards) across the field to reach the trig point on the hill top. The views are marvellous but it should be emphasized there's NO PUBLIC RIGHT OF ACCESS and you should refer to my introductory notes. Retrace your steps to the village centre and now turn left onto Loxwood Road, following it eastwards for a mile and arriving at Ifold. Turn left down Chalk Road, ignoring the first footpath sign to the right and continuing along the road to the next signed footpath going off to the right, immediately beyond the house named KOLME. Follow the path down and cross over a metalled road, going straight on down a gravel driveway and going forward to follow a narrow path to the left of a house. Continue along the path, passing a delightful lake which is over the fence on the right and going over a footbridge into a charming meadow. Now bear slightly right to cross the meadow and join a path which proceeds along the right bank of the Wey & Arun Junction Canal; you soon pass a restored lock and bridge* and continue on to reach the B2133 at Loxwood, with the very popular Onslow Arms immediately opposite. At the time of writing there was building work going on at this junction and access from the canal path onto the B2133 was impossible. If this is still the case when you do the walk you'll need to backtrack to the bridge asterisked above, cross it and continue uphill through delightful woodland along a clear path. The path swings right and keeping a clear course arrives at the B2133 by the bus stop and village shop in the centre of Loxwood; here you turn right and follow the road down to reach the Onslow Arms. From the pub, follow the B2133 south-eastwards towards Billingshurst, passing turnings to Plaistow and Kirdford, the road rising immediately beyond these turnings. Just before the brow of the hill there's a field boundary on the left at right-angles to the road, and the trig point is on the far(top) side of the field boundary roughly 80 yards from the road. However THERE IS NO PUBLIC RIGHT OF ACCESS and the only way to get into this field is over a fence OR by backtracking a little, scaling a gate immediately opposite the Kirdford turning, following the right-hand field edge parallel with the road then the near-side of the field boundary referred to above, and using a gap in the boundary hedge to get to the far side and arrive at the trig point (please refer to my introductory notes). Now retrace your steps to the bus stop in the centre of Loxwood.

East Sussex/Brighton and Hove Walks 1 - 20
South Downs Way section starts 7 - 9

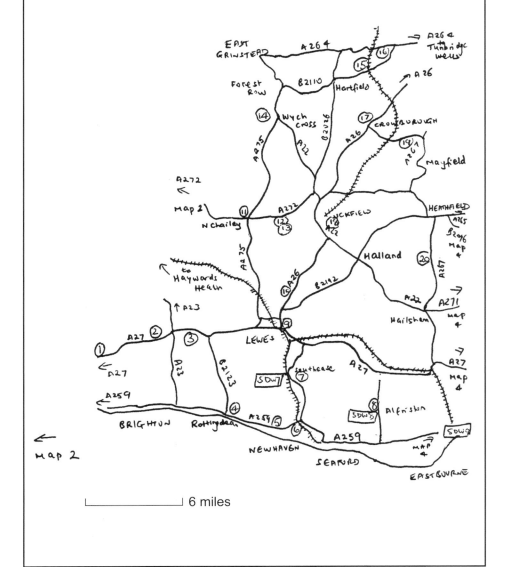

6 miles

~ PART 2 ~
WALKING THE TRIG POINTS OF EAST SUSSEX
(INCLUDING BRIGHTON & HOVE)

1 Mile Oak TQ252084 MODERATE.
Regular buses(BH) to Mile Oak from central Brighton(service 1 at the time of writing). 3.5 miles. R Mile Oak(P,S).

Your walk starts at the Mile Oak pub on Mile Oak Road, Mile Oak, near Portslade at the far north-west corner of Brighton. Continue north-westwards from the pub up Mile Oak Road to the very end, going forward to pass under the A27 road bridge then, having emerged, bear almost immediately right onto a track leading up to the Mile Oak Farm buildings. Having passed the main buildings, the track swings to the left, and you follow this track as it swings left and continues north-westwards to a T-junction with a wider track; turn right here and follow the track uphill north-eastwards, keeping the summit of Cockroost Hill to your right. Your path swings to travel just north of east, going gently downhill to reach another T-junction of paths. Turn right and follow the path south-eastwards, rising gently and arriving at the trig point at the hilltop in the adjacent field on the left, with magnificent views to Brighton and the sea. Continue along the path which veers left and drops to reach the A27 footbridge which you cross, then continue

Just a stone's throw from the busy A27 - the Mile Oak trig point

71

on the obvious path south-eastwards to pass Foredown Tower, now a countryside centre. Just beyond the tower turn right onto a signed path across a field which brings you to Fox Way; to get back to the Mile Oak pub, turn right and follow the road which turns itself into Chalky Road, descending to arrive at a T-junction with Mile Oak Road. Turn right and you'll soon be back at the pub. If you don't want to walk all the way back to the pub from Fox Way, there are plenty of buses back to Brighton from stops between there and where you started!

2 Devil's Dyke Road/Sweet Hill/Wolstonbury Hill(West Sussex) TQ280085/289097/283138 STRENUOUS.

Regular buses(BH) from Brighton serving Dyke Road Avenue junction with Tongdean Lane (services 27 and 77 at the time of writing); regular trains back serving Hassocks on Haywards Heath-Brighton line. 11 miles. R Hassocks(P,C,S); no other on-route refreshment opportunities but ample amenities in Brighton before you start.

The walk starts from the bus stop on Dyke Road Avenue at its junction with Tongdean Lane, well served by buses from Brighton (27 and 77 at the time of writing). Walk north-westwards up Dyke Road Avenue and arrive at a roundabout junction, using pavements provided to cross over the A2038; continue north-westwards across the bridge over the A27, using the pavement on the right-hand side of the bridge, and immediately arrive at another roundabout. Proceed initially anti-clockwise round it, crossing the first road (a slip road leading to the A27) but not going as far as the next exit, Devil's Dyke Road, rather bearing immediately right onto a narrow path up a steep grassy bank. When you reach the top, continue north-westwards parallel with Devil's Dyke Road which is to your left, using a choice of narrow paths to reach a car park a couple of hundred yards beyond the top of the bank. From the car park look just west of north across Devil's Dyke Road to see the first trig point of this walk on the next hillside in a field. You need to ascertain its location from here, and the point at which you need to "attack" it from the cycle path referred to below, as you will lose sight of it almost immediately. From the car park, follow a signed and very well-defined cycle track with the road towards the Dyke, then bear left to cross the road into the field that leads to the trig point. Be careful when entering the field; although at the time of writing it was manageable, watch for barbed wire in the undergrowth below you and note that in any event there is no right of access into it (please see my introductory notes). The views from the trig point are excellent, most notably to the windmill at West Blatchington to the south-east. Then retrace your steps to the cycle path and continue to follow it briefly parallel with Devil's Dyke Road. Do not, however, veer left with the path as it heads up to the road, but bear right for a few yards to join a narrow path which runs parallel with but below

Winter sunshine lights up the Devil's Dyke Road trig point

a road forking away from Devil's Dyke Road, heading northwards. Go forward to a car park, keeping a golf course to your right, and arrive at a metalled drive leading to Waterhall Golf Club. Turn right onto the drive and follow it downhill past the clubhouse and into the golf club car park. Walk through the car park to its bottom left corner, bearing left here onto an unsigned footpath, shortly reaching a T-junction and bearing left to follow a signed path downhill just west of north, keeping thick vegetation to your right and the golf course to your left. As the trees come to an end on the left, the path appears to give out with a choice of much thinner tracks left and right. Bear left here, shortly joining a clearer stony track, keeping the trees immediately to your right. Soon you're reassured by a footpath sign pointing you right; go forward to cross a stile and go downhill to the bottom of a dry valley, then haul yourself quite steeply uphill, over another stile and, as indicated by the post direction arrows, forward to a thin line of trees. Turn left here as signed through the trees, then shortly veer right uphill, again as signed, aiming for a stile* which you cross to arrive at a T-junction with a wide track. Bear briefly right here, and almost immediately you'll see the Sweet Hill trig point half-hidden in vegetation to the right of the path. The views are reasonably good, with the West Blatchington windmill particularly prominent. Now retrace your steps along this track, but rather than going back over the stile asterisked above, continue along the track to reach a crossroads of paths; go straight over and now

The Wolstonbury Hill trig point has one of the finest settings of all the Sussex trig points

downhill through a field to reach a T-junction with the South Downs Way. Bear left here along the South Downs Way through the trees, and shortly before a gate across the lane you come to a gate on the right with signed bridleways. Pass through this gate and immediately fork right to follow a clearly defined path that heads north-eastwards up onto Newtimber Hill, avoiding the temptation to veer left. Cross over Newtimber Hill then, continuing on the obvious path north-eastwards, begin descending, and thereafter drop down more steeply through a new gate past a new-build house to reach a footbridge over the A23. You are now back in West Sussex. Cross the bridge and go straight ahead along the lane which immediately veers north-westwards and becomes a rough and very muddy track heading north-westwards and contouring the lower slopes of Wolstonbury Hill. Go forward to a path junction beside a quarry which is to the left, bear hard right here onto a bridleway that heads uphill, south-eastwards, then having reached the top of the rise look out for and cross a stile in the fence on the left. Follow the path just west of north from the stile to reach the trig point atop Wolstonbury Hill, from which there are superb views in all directions most notably to the South Downs escarpment and the Jack & Jill windmills. From the trig point, head steeply downhill eastwards along a path through pasture to reach a small strip of woodland; the track goes through the strip then immediately swings left, downhill, to reach a house called the Warenne. Follow the path past the house and its gardens to reach the road onto which you turn right and which you follow to the A273. Turn right to cross the railway then bear immediately left onto a signed path that hugs the railway all the way to Hassocks; when you get to the road at the end, turn right to follow it then left to access the station.

3 Hollingbury Castle TQ321079 MODERATE.

Regular buses(BH) serving junction of Cuckmere Way and Elsted Crescent from Brighton(service 46 at the time of writing). 3 miles. R none on route although ample refreshment opportunity in Brighton generally.

This "out and back" walk starts at the bus stop by the junction of Cuckmere Way and Elsted Crescent, on the west side of Cuckmere Way (Elsted Crescent is a "name" stop on BH route 46 so simply ask to be dropped there!). Looking north from the bus stop up Cuckmere Way, turn immediately right (eastwards) off Cuckmere Way into Elsted Crescent, and follow it, but shortly before reaching a sharp left-hand bend look out for and take a narrow footpath heading to your right, uphill and south-eastwards, to reach Ditchling Road. Cross over this road and turn right to walk briefly alongside it, soon

A few minutes' bus ride from central Brighton - the Hollingbury Castle trig point

arriving at a car park entrance. Turn left to enter the car park, walk through it and then walk southwards from the car park on an obvious path that goes across open country then along the left side of an area of woodland. Keep beside the woods for a few hundred yards until you reach a sign on the right indicating you should keep to the waymarked path. Turn right here and walk up a clear path to reach a green belonging to the adjoining golf course; just above the green bear right onto a clear path which goes through the woods, then, emerging from the woods, bear left to climb to the outer perimeter of Hollingbury Castle. Bear right to follow the perimeter round to the Hollingbury Castle trig point, from which the views to the Downs and the sea are magnificent. Then retrace your steps.

4 Rottingdean/Bullock Hill/Mount Pleasant/East Brighton Golf Club TQ376025/368063/357046/345039 MODERATE.

Regular buses(BH) serving Rottingdean from Brighton. 7 miles. R Rottingdean(P,C,S), Woodingdean(P,C,S), Brighton(P,C,S).

From the very attractive centre of Rottingdean, follow the A259 coast road eastwards uphill, turning left after just over a quarter of a mile into Cranleigh Avenue, following it uphill to its end and turning right into Founthill Road. Then bear shortly left to follow Westmeston Avenue; at its end*, bear left and at oce you'll see two parallel paths going

The Bullock Hill trig point in its fine downland setting

76

Whiter than white - the Mount Pleasant trig point

off to the left. Take the left (upper) path and go forward to a gate which you will need to surmount - there is no public right of way beyong it so please refer to my introductory notes. Beyond the gate, walk along the grass initially in the same direction, rising slightly; then, continuing to rise, swing left to continue along the grass towards the backs of the houses in Westmeston Avenue with enclosures to your right and left. As you reach the highest ground, to your right there's the Rottingdean trig point in the next enclosure but one, separated from you by two barbed wire fences. It's all very private; if you try to negotiate the fencing, you're risking damage to your clothes as well as being challenged. Having viewed the trig point, retrace your steps to* above. Continue northwards beyond the end of Westmeston Avenue along a clear path that heads first just east of north then just west of north, ignoring a path going to the left and passing the remote houses marked as Balsdean Cottages. Leaving the cottages behind, go forward to a gate and continue along the path going north-westwards beyond it, passing to the right of the raised Balsdean Reservoir and soon arriving at a crossroads with a metalled track. Go straight over then keep north-westwards, the buildings of Woodingdean visible to the left and another track coming in from the left. Continue on to pass a very prominent mast, immediately beyond which there's a gap in the barbed wire*, giving you access to a field. Bear round to the right and walk uphill, passing the mast which is to your right, and continuing up to the Bullock Hill trig point. (If the gap in the fence has gone it should be possible to access the field by walking on to the next path junction a hundred yards or so further on, and entering it there. However there's no public right of way into or across this field, so please once again refer to my introductory notes.) The views from the trig point are excellent, especially to the surrounding downland. Return to the asterisked point and leave the hilltop path for good, dropping straight down via a greensward to arrive at Bexhill Road. Turn left onto this road then shortly right to follow Balsdean Road, going forward to the centre of Woodingdean past a parade of shops including a useful café. Beyond the shops go straight over the main road ahead, then walk briefly just south of west along Warren Road and go first left into Old Parish Lane. The lane becomes a path that heads southwards then bends south-eastwards and rises, with the white Mount Pleasant trig point visible ahead. As you come to the hill on which the trig point is placed, you reach a fence going off to the right, and you turn right here, just south of west, onto a path, keeping this fence to your left. Shortly a break in the fence to the left enables you to access the trig point, beautifully preserved and white-painted with lovely views to the surrounding coastline and downs. Return to the break in the fence and continue, just south of west, along the path that drops steeply to a dry valley; on reaching the valley bottom turn left at the T-junction of paths and follow the path through the valley to another T-junction. Turn left here, very soon reaching yet another T-junction, here bearing right and almost immediately reaching a fork of paths. Take the right fork which rises, passing East Brighton golf course; ascend to the hilltop, then as the ground levels out look to the

The East Brighton Golf Club trig point, with Brighton itself not far behind

left and you'll see the fourth trig point on this walk bang in the middle of the golf course to the left, with excellent views to Roedean School and the buildings of Brighton. Return to the path which now swings sharply south-west and drops down to pass through the golf club car park and arrive at a T-junction with Roedean Road. Turn right and follow this road across a set of traffic lights then bear left down Arundel Road; at the end turn right onto Marine Parade and follow it to central Brighton with its plethora of attractions.

5 Piddinghoe/Telscombe TQ427029/398037 MODERATE.
Numerous and regular buses(BH) serving Peacehaven and Telscombe Tye on Brighton-Newhaven route. 5.5 miles. R Peacehaven(P,C,S).

The walk starts at the junction of the main A259 South Coast Road with Piddinghoe Avenue in Peacehaven, just over half a mile east of the roundabout junction with Sutton Avenue in the village centre. Walk just east of north from the A259 up Piddinghoe Avenue, going straight over Arundel Road and continuing on a metalled road towards some buildings. It looks like a dead end but just before you reach the buildings you're able to turn left and follow a path which proceeds northwards across fields to a T-junction with a metalled road. Turn right onto that road past Lower Hodden Farm, the road bending slightly left to pass the farm buildings, and rising gently. On reaching the brow of the hill it bends slightly right and gently descends to arrive at the Piddinghoe trig point a few hundred yards beyond this bend, with good views from here to the Ouse valley. Retrace your steps to the bend where you need to turn right onto a clear path that proceeds due west in a straight line to a junction with Telscombe Road, then walk westwards on along Telscombe Road. This is tedious walking and you could be forgiven for hopping one of the many buses that ply this stretch of road! As the road bends south-west, don't bend south-west with it but join an obvious albeit badly pot-holed bridlepath which heads north-westwards; soon you leave the housing behind and rise gently, then at the top of the rise your track swings sharply right to arrive at a metalled road* from which there are excellent views to the very pretty village of Telscombe (not to be confused with Telscombe Cliffs). Walk briefly down the metalled road but just before the cattle grid bear left onto a signed, very obvious path that heads north-westwards, the ground falling away steeply just to the right, your path aiming for an isolated hilltop house. You reach a fence and gate, just beyond which you bear right onto a clear path that goes past the house (keeping it to the left) heading just west of north, and soon you reach what looks like a very complex array of gates. Go through the gate actually on the path then bear immediately left, uphill, keeping a wire fence to your right and heading for some works with a wire enclosure. You will spot the Telscombe trig point within the enclosure very close to the wire, on the north-east side, but you need to walk round to the south side of the enclosure for the best views. Retrace your steps all the

A wiry prison for the Telscombe trig point

way back to the metalled road leading down to Telscombe, and walk up to the start of the metalled road asterisked above. Don't retrace your steps back down to Telscombe Road but go forward onto a very obvious path that proceeds south-westwards along the hilltop, then descends steadily. Although there are fields immediately to your right and left there are huge sprawls of housing in both directions beyond the fields. In due course you arrive at the A259 at a spot called Telscombe Tye from which you have lots of options: you could bear left to walk beside the A259 all the way back to Peacehaven, you could start to do this then at the Badgers Watch pub bear right to follow a clifftop path back to Peacehaven, you could catch a bus back to Peacehaven from the bus stop immediately adjacent, or you could catch a bus on the other side of the road to the pretty village of Rottingdean or on to Brighton. There's another trig point walk which starts at Rottingdean(described in walk 4 above), if this one on its own has not satisfied you!

6 Meeching Down, Newhaven TQ438010 MODERATE.
Regular buses(BH) serving Newhaven from Brighton. 1 mile. R Newhaven(P,C,S).

From the top of Newhaven High Street cross straight over the inner ring road but instead of continuing up the main A259 Brighton road fork just left of that road onto Church Hill. Walk up Church Hill south-westwards, ignoring side turnings, the surface becoming rougher, and go forward onto the green of Meeching Down Open Space, with thick vegetation to the right. Look out for a footpath junction sign on the left about halfway across the green, but a little before you get level with it, look out for and follow a path going off right into the thick vegetation. Walk through the trees, ignoring the first path going off to the right, and soon you will see the trig point a little further along off the path to the right, nestling in the woods with sadly no views to speak of. Retrace your steps down Church Hill to the town.

The Meeching Down trig point, in thick woodland

7 Tarring Neville/Denton/Rookery Hill
TQ446036/458024/467008 MODERATE.
Regular trains serving Southease and Bishopstone on Lewes-Seaford line. 4.5 miles. R Bishopstone(P,S).

The walk starts at Southease station from which you head westwards along the track (South Downs Way), soon reaching the Ouse where you turn left to follow the left bank. In half a mile or so you reach a stile just beyond which you drop down the bank to turn left onto a path that goes eastwards to reach the A26; turn right to follow this very busy main road, soon reaching the hamlet of Tarring Neville to your left. Turn left here onto a lane that goes past the pretty village church, and arrive at a T-junction with another

The Tarring Neville trig point, with the pretty village church just down the hill

A green expanse stretches ahead behind the Denton trig point

lane. Cross straight over at the T-junction to a gate, pass through the gate and head south-eastwards uphill through the field to the Tarring Neville trig point from which there are good views to Newhaven and the mouth of the Ouse, although the church of Tarring Neville provides the most attractive aspect. Now return to the lane, turn left and walk back to the A26, bearing left to continue beside the road, in a few hundred yards reaching South Heighton. Ignore the first signed road into South Heighton but continue to the next one, Heighton Road; turn left and follow it initially north-east, very soon swinging south-east uphill, then south-west, then sharp left, eastwards and downhill past a church to a T-junction with Denton Road. Turn right into Denton Road then almost immediately left, uphill on a steep footpath. At the top, don't turn right into King's Avenue but continue in the same direction, bearing left into The Crescent and very soon swinging right into Fairholme Road. Almost immediately, however, turn left off Fairholme Road onto a signed bridleway, and follow it for a couple of hundred yards to a tall telegraph mast; bear right immediately before it to enter a field and go forward to the Denton trig point from which there are great views to Seaford Head and the sea. Return to the bridleway, turn left and retrace your steps along it very briefly, then bear left onto a signed path that brings you back to Fairholme Road. Turn left and follow it downhill to its end, then bear right into Palmerston Road and go second left into Falaise Road. This peters out but you continue in the same direction on a good path, initially downhill then uphill onto an escarpment; although the map shows a number of paths diverging, keep to an obvious path that heads south-eastwards with

Barbed wire protection for the Rookery Hill trig point

the ground falling away to the left and housing to the right. The views back to Newhaven and the Ouse valley are tremendous. Still keeping to the highest ground and proceeding south-eastwards, you soon reach the third trig point on this walk, Rookery Hill, the trig point itself just the other side of the barbed wire on the right. There are again super views to Newhaven and its harbour, and northwards to the Downs and the beautiful church of Old Bishopstone, its tower similar to that at Tarring Neville. Now walk downhill on the clear signed path to arrive at a metalled road and turn right to follow it to a T-junction with Newhaven Road, at which you turn left. (A footpath just before the T-junction cuts the corner). Follow Newhaven Road briefly then cross it and turn first right, signposted Bishopstone Station, turning first left into Hawth Hill then first right onto Station Road, and follow it to the station.

8 Norton Top/Camp Hill/Frog Firle TQ487033/496014/509011
STRENUOUS.
Reasonably regular buses serving Alfriston from Berwick(ESCC) and on Berwick-Seaford route(CCB). 7.5 miles. R Alfriston (P,C,S).

Your walk starts in Alfriston. Leave Alfriston by walking up Star Lane westwards from the Star Inn on the main street, following the South Downs Way; go forward into Kings Ride and keep walking uphill on the South Downs Way, following the national trail signposts. Continue to gain height and follow the top of the escarpment, enjoying splendid views to the north, and in two miles from Alfriston reaching the Bo Peep Bostal car park and a footpath signpost with paths pointing left to Denton and High And Over. You need to take the latter path, which heads clearly south-westwards then swings southwards and provides lovely ridgetop walking. As you head south, you can see a hill ahead with a trig point very conspicuously perched on top of it and, reaching the base of this hill, you see a kissing gate to your right. Leave the main ridgetop path, go through the kissing gate and climb the hill, using a stile to take you into the next field and enabling you to access the trig point at Norton Top; the views are superb, northwards to the Downs and southwards to a line of coast extending from Newhaven Harbour to the Seven Sisters. Retrace your steps to the main ridgetop path and continue to follow it, the ground falling away steeply to the left, but don't be sucked downhill, making sure you keep to the top of the escarpment. Ignore a right fork going away across a golf course but keep to the main path, going through an area of trees, on emerging from which you'll see a signed bridlepath* forking left. Although you'll need to take this, which continues on the ridgetop, you first need to bear right, almost opposite the turning, into a field, and follow the right-hand field edge to arrive shortly at the Camp Hill trig point, half hidden in the trees. This is a disappointment, with no views to speak of! Retrace your steps and now take the asterisked path which soon arrives at Alfriston Road; it's

Don't fence me in.....the Frog Firle trig point

impossible to cut the corner, and you need to go to the very end, bearing right here onto Alfriston Road and following it uphill. A little way past the brow of the hill is a car park and information board, and just beyond the car park is a field which can easily be accessed and in which, by the roadside, is the Frog Firle trig point. The views are limited from this trig point, but by returning to the car park and following the metalled path heading south-east away from the car park and through the trees, you arrive at a splendid viewpoint looking across the Cuckmere valley. Now follow the clear albeit narrow path very very steeply downhill, using steps where provided; take care as this is an almost vertical hillside, and you should refrain from rushing and watch where you're putting your feet. In due course you arrive at the valley floor, and you now need to join the left bank of the Cuckmere heading upstream (left), although it is possible to cut this corner by walking across the pasture. When you reach the bank, follow it upstream for just over a mile to reach Alfriston, although there is the option of a bridge crossing to use the right bank which gives you access to the pretty village of Litlington. On arrival at Alfriston, the riverside path - whichever bank you choose - passes the church, and immediately beyond the church you bear left to access the church green from which there is an obvious path taking you back to the village centre. There is no shortage of amenities including several excellent eating places.

9 Lewes/Cliffe TQ 401091/ 434107 MODERATE,

STRENUOUS IN PLACES.
**Regular trains to Lewes from Brighton, Seaford, Eastbourne and London. 5 miles.
R Lewes (P,C,S).**

This is two walks for the price of one and can be done in one go or in two - perhaps one
before Sunday lunch in Lewes, and one after! From the Lewes station entrance, turn
left over the bridge then bear right into Priory Street and go forward into and along the
delightful Southover High Street. At the top of this street go over the mini-roundabout
junction with Bell Lane, then as the main road bends left, go straight on into Juggs
Road. This narrow metalled lane rises, going just south of west, then swings sharply left
to reach a footbridge high over the A27; cross the footbridge then, still on Juggs Road,
bear right to proceed uphill, more or less parallel with the A27. You swing from walking
just south of west to walk in a more south-westerly direction and soon reach Old Mill
House on your left and Downsview immediately opposite on your right*. Continue
along the path, keeping a field** to your left; the path now gets a bit rougher, and shortly
arrives at a gate, with open fields ahead. You need to go through the gate then turn
immediately hard left into the field double-asterisked above, but please note that there
is no public right of way into this field and you should refer to my introductory notes.
To reach the Lewes trig point, climb to the highest point in the field, and you will be
rewarded with excellent views from the pillar to Lewes, Mount Caburn, the Ouse Valley
and the South Downs. Retrace your steps all the way back to the SINGLE-asterisked
point above, and turn left past Downsview to go forward to a signed path; follow this
path just north of west steeply downhill, aiming for a kissing gate and the footbridge
over the A27. Cross the bridge on the obvious path and continue on under the railway,
going forward to a T-junction with the A277. Turn right to follow beside this road uphill,
and go straight over the traffic light controlled crossroads at the top, continuing along
the High Street into the centre of Lewes; if you're happy to call it a day here, turn right
into Station Street (again controlled by traffic lights) and keep straight ahead to reach
the station.

To reach a further trig point from Lewes, on what is an "out and back" walk, stay on the
High Street and keep on downhill. Cross the road*** at the bottom of the hill to enter
the modern precinct and go forward to the bridge crossing over the River Ouse, then,
from the bridge, walk eastwards along Cliffe High Street to its end. Go straight over
into Chapel Hill and follow it south-eastwards uphill; just before you reach a sign for
Lewes Golf Club turn left onto a little metalled spur road, then bear right onto a signed
path that proceeds steeply uphill through woodland, emerging onto a golf course. Now
follow the footpath marker posts, observing the yellow arrow signs carefully, uphill across
the golf course, heading just north of east, and being careful to look out for golf balls -
signs tell you which way to look! Having kept to the path signs, you get within a few

yards of a stile over the golf course boundary fence, but just before the fence you need to turn left onto a metalled path that goes uphill again, passing more of the golf course. Shortly you reach two stiles close together in fencing to your right. Bear right to cross the first stile then continue uphill, aiming for the hilltop, and you will reach the Cliffe trig point; the views on a clear day are sensational, with a massive 360 degree panorama of Lewes, the Downs, the Ouse valley, the Cuckmere valley and the sea. Then retrace your steps to Lewes - it's downhill all the way!! The quickest way back to the station is to turn left at the triple-asterisked road crossing and walk up Friars Walk to the crossroads with Station Road, here turning left to reach the station.

10 Ringmer TQ446142 EASY.

Regular buses(ESCC) serving Barcombe Cross from Lewes; regular buses(BH) serving A26 Barcombe Lane turning on Brighton-Tunbridge Wells route; regular buses(BH) serving Ringmer from Lewes. 3.5 miles maximum, 2.5 miles minimum. R Barcombe Cross(P,S), Ringmer(P,S).

This walk starts from the car park on Barcombe Lane at Barcombe Mills, a mile or so south-east of Barcombe Cross; for bus travellers from Barcombe Cross it can be reached by following Barcombe Mills Road south-eastwards for about a mile, and for bus travellers from the A26 it can be reached by leaving the bus at the Barcombe Lane stop and following the lane north-westwards for about half a mile. Alternatively, it can be joined on to walk 12(Newick) as described below. From the road entrance to the car park turn right and make for the top left-hand corner of the car park, passing through a gate, walking along a rather narrow overgrown path and then going through another gate into a field. Head eastwards through the field, keeping the attractive stream and falls immediately to your left. You reach a farm lane onto which you turn left and which you follow briefly, then just before the gate turn right onto a signed path, entering a field; follow the left-hand field edge and at the sharp corner bear left as signed with the field edge. Having rounded the corner, now walk diagonally across the field to a gate which you go through, then walk straight ahead through an overgrown field to a stile. Cross the stile - be warned that it can be very muddy hereabouts - and very shortly bear right across a plank bridge then left to proceed south-eastwards along the right-hand field edge to a gate and, shortly beyond that, the crossing of the A26. Cross with great care, bear right and then almost immediately left up the drive signposted Clayhill House. Keeping the wooden garages immediately to your left and the house to your right, go straight on to a green path - it looks like a private garden but it is a right of way - and continue to just short of a gate. Don't go through the gate but just before it bear left onto a narrow path that proceeds over a stile and through some vegetation. Proceeding in the same direction, emerge into more open country and continue south-eastwards uphill on a wider path to reach the Ringmer trig point which offers lovely views to the Downs. You could simply backtrack from here if you're pushed for time, but if you want to continue to Ringmer, go forward to the path crossing just beyond the trig point; don't turn left or right but go straight on, veering in a slightly more easterly direction. You pass through an overgrown field on what is a rather ill-defined path, aiming for trees ahead, and, keeping a line of vegetation to your right, descend to reach the trees. When you get to the trees, enter the woods on the obvious path (there's another a bit further down to the left - don't be tempted onto this), and follow the path which proceeds very pleasantly through woods and goes forward to a lane. Keep going along the lane to a T-junction with a road onto which you turn right and which you follow for a mile or so into Ringmer from which there are regular buses to Lewes.

11 North Chailey TQ388215 EASY.
Regular buses serving North Chailey on Lewes-Newick route(ESCC) and on Haywards Heath-Uckfield route(CL). 1 mile. R none.

From the junction of the A272 and A275 at North Chailey, head westwards along the A272 past the (redundant) church then turn right up the signed approach road to North Chailey windmill. Just before reaching the windmill and its neighbouring buildings turn right onto a track and shortly left onto a path that goes past the right-hand side of the

Peeping out from the bracken - the North Chailey trig point

buildings. Beyond the buildings you reach a path crossroads; turn right here, and then bear shortly right again onto a path that soon brings you to the trig point, from which there are superb views northwards to Ashdown Forest. Continue from the trig point along the path and reach a T-junction with a wider path onto which you turn right and which you follow (ignoring a left turn just past a large house), enjoying splendid views through the trees to the distant Downs. You soon arrive back at the A272, bearing left to return to the start.

12 Newick TQ422200 MODERATE.

Regular buses serving Newick from Lewes(ESCC) and on Haywards Heath-Uckfield route(CL); regular buses(BH) serving Isfield on Lewes-Uckfield route. 3.5 miles. R Newick(P,S), Isfield(P,C).

This walk follows the signed Ouse Valley Way throughout. Facing outwards from the bus shelter at Newick on the green, turn left to follow the main A272 briefly eastwards but then take the first road turning right; you pass the edge of the green and the Bull pub then continue south-eastwards along the road for just under three quarters of a mile. You arrive at a lane to the left opposite Founthill Cottage, and need to turn left up this lane and follow it until it shortly reaches a right-hand bend, at which you leave the road and go straight on (still south-eastwards) over a stile as signed. You bear right and pass through a gateway into a second field, then follow the left-hand field edge south-eastwards, almost immediately seeing the trig point on a hillock to the right, surrounded by nettles! The views out towards Ashdown Forest are delightful. Pass a gate, a small wood and a pond on the left, and carry on towards barns to arrive at a rough farm track, turning right onto the track to shortly reach the farm drive, and cross the stile on the left into the field. Follow the right-hand field edge to the field end, then turn right through the gate into a further field and continue along the left-hand field edge briefly to a stile on the left. Cross the stile and enter the field on the left (ignoring the stile on the right going into woods) then follow the right-hand field edge with the wood on the right. At the wood's end you carry on across the field to a farm gate leading into a lane, turning right very briefly then left up the bank to a stile, going forward into a field. Turn left and follow the left-hand field edge with a little wood to the left. At the end of the wood continue half right across a field, aiming for farm buildings; upon reaching the house on the right, pass to the left of it, following the garden boundary, then at the end of the garden bear right onto a grassy track between an oast house to the left and Vuggles Farm to the right. Cross a small bridge and carry on to the end of the wall and farm gate, then turn left and follow a rough track along a right-hand field edge, going forward to reach a farm gate and stile. You turn right into the meadow towards a metal farm gate, going forward to enter another meadow; now cross a ditch and turn right, following

The Newick trig point on a nettle-clad hillside

the ditch, to a gap between the Ouse to your left and another channel to the right. You go over the next meadow to meet the river again, and as you get there it's worth detouring to visit a magnificent weir to the left via a stile. Back on the Ouse Valley Way, you rise briefly to reach a track which you follow for a couple of hundred yards then, continuing to keep the Ouse to your left, you turn left as signposted onto a riverside path through the meadows, going forward to White Bridge. Turn left to cross the bridge and follow a track towards Isfield. You could easily make a walking link with the Ringmer trig point walk (walk 10 above) by turning immediately right once having crossed White Bridge, to follow the left bank of the Ouse for 2.5 miles all the way to Barcombe Mills and its car park, the location of which is described in walk 10 above. However, if you want to stop at Isfield, just keep on the track having crossed White Bridge, and you'll arrive in the village with pub, occasional café and excellent bus links.

13 Fletching/Camp Hill Clump/Gills Lap
TQ 433237/469289/469319 STRENUOUS.
Regular buses serving Newick on Haywards Heath-Uckfield route (CL) and from Lewes(ESCC); regular buses(MB) serving Hartfield on Tunbridge Wells-Three Bridges-Crawley route; Haywards Heath and Three Bridges can be linked by rail, as can Lewes and Three Bridges. 11.5 miles. R Newick(P,S), Fletching (P,S), Duddleswell(C), Hartfield(P,C,S).

Your walk starts in the centre of Newick by the shop at the west end of the green on the north side of the main road. Take the lane leading north-west away from the main road just left (west) of the shop going forward shortly to a narrow metalled path with a sign prohibiting cyclists. Follow the metalled path up to a road and turn right to follow the road briefly then bear right again along Alexander Mead; continue along the lane leading towards the sewage works then just before the gate to the works turn left along the right-hand field edge. The path swings to the right just beyond the works then left, downhill, to the edge of some woods. Bear left here then shortly right along a boardwalk through marshy ground and under a line of pylons, going forward to emerge from the marsh into a field, and it's now straightforward going along a clear track just north of east in the Ouse valley. You arrive at a road at Fletching Mill Bridge; turn right to follow the road, crossing the Ouse and ascending to the pretty village of Fletching. Turn left at the T-junction and walk past the church which is to your right. Immediately beyond the church turn right to walk along the back of the churchyard eastwards on an obvious path, keeping on to the far eastern end of the churchyard and turning left to reach a path junction on a field corner. Take the path heading north-eastwards across the field and go straight on into the next field, the path clearly defined between the crops. At the end you arrive at a rather overgrown track. Turn left to follow the track north-westwards, until the vegetation on your left relents to provide a view to the Fletching trig point across the field to your left, although to access it you'll need to surmount the

The spire of Fletching church is just visible beyond the Fletching trig point

barbed wire fence, there being no public right of way into the field(please refer to introductory notes). From the trig point, if you decide to access it, there are lovely views back to Newick and the Downs. Retrace your steps and this time continue along the track which veers to the left and downhill; in due course it peters out and a footpath sign directs you to the right, the path going across a field but reasonably clearly defined on the ground. You go forward to a strip of woodland, entering it and dropping down to a footbridge, then go steeply up again. You proceed over the next field north-eastwards - again it can be discerned on the ground - and cross to a further field, descending to a valley meadow. Veer right as you reach the valley bottom, a signpost directing you to and through a wooded area and past buildings to reach a road. Cross straight over onto a path that proceeds over a field between electric fences then veers right beside trees and keeping the field boundary to your right. Go forward to reach a track and then a T-junction of driveways. Turn left and immediately right to pass through a modern wooden gate and, beyond the gate, along a path to reach a road; turn left onto the road and follow it, in just over a quarter of a mile taking the next right turn, Picketts Lane, and walking along it to the A22. On reaching it cross with care, turn right and almost immediately bear left along a pleasant country road to reach a T-junction. Turn right

The Camp Hill Clump trig point in the heart of Ashdown Forest

and follow the road briefly, then as it bends right at Boringwheel Mill Farm, turn left up a signed path, entering Ashdown Forest. Now follow the very obvious path which heads uphill, initially north-eastwards, veering north-west before veering north-east again with superb views across the forest. Ignore all crossing tracks. Once on the hilltop you pass houses and reach a T-junction with a driveway; turn right and follow it, but when the main driveway swings sharply right carry on in the same direction past Little Gassons. When you reach a path fork shortly beyond Little Gassons, take the right-hand fork, then just before this path enters the wood, turn right onto a path going uphill to a T-junction with a wider track. Turn left here and very shortly reach another T-junction, turning right here and arriving at the B2026 road at Duddleswell. Turn left to follow it past

The Gills Lap trig point - or Galleons Lap for Winnie The Pooh fans

the popular tea room and garden centre and go on to a road junction; immediately opposite New Road, signed Crowborough, turn left onto a track and very shortly reach a group of trees called Camp Hill Clump with a trig point just to the left, commanding spectacular views. Pass to the left of the clump with Wealdway signs, then, at the crossroads of paths immediately beyond, you turn right to follow a very wide path initially north-east, then just west of north, then north. This is the course of the Wealdway and the views are superb. Reaching the B2026 again, cross straight over then at the path crossroads very shortly beyond turn left, now on the Vanguard Way, following the track and descending to a T-junction of paths; turn left and ignoring the veering of a path to the right, go straight up to the junction of Chuck Hatch Road and Kidds Hill. Cross over and walk between these two roads to a carpark/picnic area with two prominent clumps of trees. Pass to the right of them and aim up the hillside, going forward to a clear track which climbs, levelling out with the lovely trees of Gills Lap (Galleons Lap for Pooh fans!) to the right. The track descends a little and the trig point here can be seen just off the track to the right, beautifully situated in woodland. Now continue on along the track, passing a quarry and car park, enjoying great views across the forest to your left; sticking to the main track, descend to enter woodland and arrive at a T-junction with a road. Turn left to follow it then in just over a quarter of a mile take the first road turning off to the right. The road descends and shortly bends left, then just beyond the bend turn right onto a signed bridlepath that takes you down to the rebuilt (1999) Poohsticks Bridge, in an idyllic woodland setting. Expect company! Cross it and continue up to a fork with metalled lanes going straight on and to the right; go straight on then when the lane veers left at a gate, take the signed path northwards keeping trees to the left. Follow the path as signed, veering north-eastwards uphill and away from the trees, enjoying lovely views back to Ashdown Forest. Once on the hilltop go forward to the field corner by some buildings and turn right onto the path signed Hartfield. You pass the imposing buildings of Galleypot Hill Farm which are to your left, with paddocks for horses to your right, and in a few hundred yards you reach a path junction with the left-hand path signed for "village." Take this path which soon reaches a bridge - declared dangerous at the time of writing, so detour briefly round it! - then beyond the bridge continue northwards on the obvious path downhill, with lovely views to the church spire at Hartfield. You arrive at the B2110 road, turn right onto it and follow it for a few hundred yards to reach journey's end in the very pretty village of Hartfield with a good range of amenities.

14 Hindleap TQ404324 MODERATE.

Regular but not very frequent buses(EB) serving Wych Cross on Eastbourne-East Grinstead route. 3.5 miles maximum, 2 miles minimum. R Wych Cross(C).

A huge swathe of Ashdown Forest can be seen from the Hindleap trig point

From the Wych Cross traffic lights walk westwards on the West Hoathly / Sharpthorne road passing the Twyford Lane turning/car park/picnic area which is to your left, and continuing for just over a quarter of a mile beyond that to the next car park/picnic area; turn left into it and look to your right (westwards) and you'll see the Hindleap trig point, a rich brown colour, with delightful views across Ashdown Forest. Leaving the trig point you should make for the interpretation panel in the car park and head downhill from there; you soon arrive at a crossroads of paths, turning left by the bench and following a delightful path which enters woods and climbs up to the Twyford Lane car park. Here you could just retrace your steps back to Wych Cross, but for a longer walk, actually the Hindleap Circular Walk, turn sharply right just before the Twyford Lane car park and walk steeply downhill parallel with Twyford Lane. At the next fork, go right by a holly tree and follow the path downhill between beech and holly trees to a stream at the valley bottom; cross the stream over a sleeper bridge and continue uphill, going straight ahead and ignoring the first turning you come to on the right. At the next fork turn right uphill between the trees to arrive back on open heath, go forward to a T-junction where you turn left, and then almost at once fork right up the slope across the grass, continuing back to the car park. You could either follow the road back to Wych Cross, or do the first part of the circular walk again as far as Twyford Lane car park/picnic area, bearing left here onto Twyford Lane then right to follow the road just over half a mile back to Wych Cross. A café is to be found in the garden centre that lies immediately adjacent to the A22 at Wych Cross.

15 Withyham TQ511356 MODERATE.

Regular buses(MB) serving Withyham and Hartfield on Tunbridge Wells-East Grinstead-Three Bridges route. 6 miles maximum, 3.5 miles minimum. R Withyham(P), Hartfield(P,C,S).

From the pub in Withyham, head eastwards along the Tunbridge Wells road and soon bear left along Station Road, signed Balls Green and Blackham; follow this the short distance to Balls Green and in the centre of the village turn right along the road that is actually named Ball's Green. Follow it eastwards to its end and here join a path that heads uphill, south-eastwards, the line of the path very clear, the views to the Medway valley quite delightful. You cross into a further field, continuing in the same direction to reach the Withyham-Tunbridge Wells road* which you cross over, then continue on the path the other side, heading just north of east as signed. As you reach a field boundary, go past the boundary hedge then veer just south of east along the right-hand field edge to arrive at the Hunt's Farm buildings which you keep to your left; pass the buildings and continue along the path as signed south-eastwards, going forward to the next field boundary. Turn right immediately beyond the hedge to follow the right-hand field edge and follow it to the Withyham trig point which is just beside the path to the left, with lovely views to the surrounding countryside. Now you have a choice. You could go forward the short distance to the road junction, turn right and follow the road, Ladies Mile, down to a T-junction, bearing left here and proceeding back to Withyham. A more interesting option is to retrace your steps from the trig point to the path/road junction as asterisked above; turn right onto the road and follow it for just under a mile to reach a crossing of the old East Grinstead-Tunbridge Wells railway. Bear left just short of the crossing to join the Forest Way path - actually the course of the old

Fair waved the golden corn - the Withyham trig point

railway - and follow it back to Balls Green, here turning left to follow the road back to the village centre and go forward from there to Withyham the way you came. Alternatively, you could remain on the Forest Way for a mile and a half to reach the pretty village of Hartfield.

16 Blackham TQ484392 MODERATE.

Regular trains serving Ashurst on London Victoria-Oxted-Uckfield line. 6 miles maximum, 3.5 miles minimum. R Sussex Oak(P).

If you're reliant on public transport, you'll have to endure a fair amount of unavoidable road walking for this expedition. Turn left out of Ashurst station then turn left again to join the A264 East Grinstead-Tunbridge Wells road and follow it for just over a mile to the Sussex Oak pub, a welcome oasis as there are no buses along this section. From the pub continue uphill, woodland now to your left; the road levels out, but as it begins to lose height and veer slightly right, just over a quarter of a mile from the pub, look out for and take a track going off to the left uphill. There's no signpost here but a footpath sign about 100 yards up the track reassures you and directs you right, through the trees, to a stile at the far end. Cross the stile and turn left to follow a left-hand field edge, going downhill and passing under a line of pylons. At the bottom of the field shortly beyond the pylons, turn left into the adjacent field and now follow the left-hand field edge round, keeping the pylons to the left. Climb up and pass through into the next field, walking roughly parallel with the pylons, and keep walking across the top of the field in a north-easterly direction to reach the Blackham trig point from which there are beautiful views down to the Medway valley. Retrace your steps now to the Sussex Oak pub. You could just walk back to Ashurst the way you came, but for a more interesting walk, turn right just beyond the pub onto Beech Green Road and follow it for a mile and a half to a sharp right-hand bend with a signpost for Hale Court Farm on the corner by a lovely tile-hung house. Turn hard left here onto the metalled Hale Court Farm drive, and continue along it, northwards, swinging eastwards (observing the Hale Court Farm signs) and ignoring the path going straight ahead. Descend, passing another beautiful house which is to your left and continuing to the point where the field to the left, adjoining this house, ends. Turn left here onto a path heading north-west; again there's no intial signpost, but soon a path sign reassures you, and you walk downhill through an orchard and across a signed path junction to a footbridge just south-east of Blackham Court. Once over the bridge turn right onto a signed path which proceeds clearly north-eastwards across fields to arrive at the River Medway. Now follow the left bank of the Medway past the weir all the way to the A264, turn right to follow beside the road and almost at once you'll find yourself back in Ashurst.

A fine Wealden panorama from the Blackham trig point

17 Crowborough TQ512308 MODERATE.

Regular buses(BH) serving Crowborough on Brighton-Tunbridge Wells route. 4 miles maximum, 0.8 miles minimum. R Crowborough(P,S).

The sad graffiti-plastered trig point at Crowborough

Your walk starts at Crowborough Cross where the main A26 Uckfield-Tunbridge Wells meets the B2100 coming in from Rotherfield, right in the centre of the very sprawling village of Crowborough. From here follow the A26 Beacon Road south-westwards for just under half a mile, looking out for a tall very obvious mast on the left; just before you reach the mast, pass through a gate to enter a complex containing not only mast but water tower, and in this complex is the Crowborough trig point. At the time of writing it was in an appalling state of repair with graffiti plastered all over it.

Although you could just retrace your steps, I recommend you continue south-westwards along the A26 for just over half a mile more and you'll reach the clubhouse of Crowborough Beacon Golf Club. From here there are quite fantastic views southwards and you can enjoy a lovely walk using the paths and bridleways across the golf course; you could simply follow the golf course round using the paths available, noting the hole numbers 1-18 marked on each tee as indicators of progress and location! You don't even need to walk all the way back to the trig point or Crowborough Cross either, as buses stop very close to the clubhouse on both sides of the A26.

18 Uckfield Quarry TQ475199 EASY.

Regular buses(BH) serving the Highlands pub on Brighton-Tunbridge Wells route. 0.25 miles. R Uckfield(P,C,S), Ridgewood(P).

This is a very short walk, perhaps working well as a post-lunch stroll from the Highlands pub immediately south of the roundabout junction at Ridgewood on the southern edge of Uckfield; to reach the roundabout from Uckfield station, turn left out of the station and just follow the road (High Street) in a straight line a little east of south for about half a mile. From the bus stop outside the pub (the pub to your left) cross over the road, and, heading westwards, follow a metalled driveway signed Ridgewood Manor, a rest home. A short distance down this driveway, turn left through a very rusty metalled gate into a rather overgrown field and walk in a straight line up to the right-hand edge of the trees marking the top end of Uckfield Quarry , a truly rural area despite its name; the trig point can be found in the edge of the trees. Having found it, and enjoyed the tranquillity of this spot, retrace your steps to enjoy a drink at the pub.

19 Argos Hill TQ570283 EASY.

Regular buses(EB) serving Rotherfield on Tunbridge Wells-Eastbourne route. 3.5 miles maximum, 2.5 miles minimum. R Rotherfield (P,C,S).

This walk, which follows roads throughout, starts in the very pretty village of Rotherfield. Leave the village by walking southwards along the B2101 South Street which veers first south-westwards then south-eastwards; keep on this road for just over a mile (from Rotherfield) and shortly beyond the buildings of Burwood which are on the left, bear right onto a narrow minor road, shortly arriving at a crossroads. Go straight over the crossroads and along the road eastwards and you'll very shortly see the imposing Argos Hill windmill which is to your left. At the time of writing this old post mill, dating from about 1835, was undergoing what appeared to be extensive remedial work, with the whole structure covered up and accompanied by scaffolding; you'll see also that the mill is only accessible by going briefly up a gravel drive clearly marked Private and then bearing right into a private back garden. The trig point can be seen immediately adjacent to the mill, also in the garden. It would be wholly inappropriate to venture into the garden without seeking permission, and you should refer to my introductory notes, but even if you don't go up to the trig point you can still enjoy fine views southwards from the road here. Now you've a choice. Although you could just retrace your steps to Rotherfield there is another possibility which provides another glimpse back to the past. Retrace your steps to the B2101, turn left and then take the first right turn into Sheriff's Lane, following it to a T-junction with Yew Tree Lane; turn left here and walk along Yew Tree Lane parallel with the course of the old Polegate-Eridge railway line to the left, and indeed you may like, where the opportunity arises, to climb up onto the embankment to get more of a feel of the line. Continue along Yew Tree Lane to a T-junction with the B2100 Mark Cross-Rotherfield road, from which your way is left, back to Rotherfield along the B2100, beginning with your going under the site of the old railway bridge crossing. However by detouring up the road to the right immediately before the site of the crossing you can inspect the magnificently restored old Rotherfield station, now a very impressive private dwelling. Walk to Rotherfield along the B2100 to complete the circle.

20 Horam/Cross-in-Hand TQ 563158/558217 MODERATE.

Regular buses(EB) serving Horam and Cross-in-Hand on Tunbridge Wells-Eastbourne route. 8 miles maximum, 5.5 miles minimum. R Horam(P,C,S), Heathfield(P,C,S).

Starting from the A267 at Horam, follow the A267 south-westwards, bearing first right onto the road signposted for the golf course and Chiddingly, following this road for about half a mile then bearing first right onto a minor road. Look out in a couple of hundred yards for the signpost for Stonehill Farm on the left, and a little way past that, on the right, is a driveway signposted Squirrels. Immediately beyond Squirrels is a gated track leading off to the right and by following this track - it is private, so please refer to my introductory notes - you will very shortly reach the Horam trig point half hidden in bushes on the right. Return to the road and turn right, following it for another couple of hundred yards then turn right onto a (plinth) signed bridleway signed Stream Mill; this descends, veers a little right to pass the mill and continues over the stream then swings north-westwards to arrive at a minor road. Turn right onto the road and follow it for just over half a mile, with woodland to the right. Shortly beyond Copford Farm on the right, look out for and climb steps leading into the woods on the right, go over a stile and follow a crude path through the woods, then emerge from the woods and

A glorious view awaits at the Cross-in-Hand trig point

continue in the direction signed, just north of east. As you go through the field, head for the higher ground you see to the left, making for the highest point and passing directly between the two clumps of woodland; from here, descend steeply to a stile, clearly signed, cross the stream and another stile, then continue uphill aiming for the farm buildings ahead. Pass to the left of the buildings as signed to reach a T-junction with the farm approach road and enjoy fine views back the way you've come. Turn left onto the farm road and reach a T-junction with a metalled road, turning right to follow it and reach a T-junction with the A267; bear left to follow the A267 for just under half a mile, taking care as this is a busy road, then at the crossroads turn right onto West Street Lane and follow it for just over a quarter of a mile to reach a right fork*. You now have two options. You could take the right fork to shortly reach the Cuckoo Trail(the old Polegate-Heathfield railway) and turn right to follow it back to Horam, from where you could catch a bus to Cross-in-Hand. For a longer walk, continue along West Street Lane from the asterisked point to reach the Cuckoo Trail and, having accessed it, follow it for a mile and a half into Heathfield as signed. On reaching the main street in Heathfield, you need to turn left to follow the A267 into Cross-in-Hand, although it's hardly exciting walking and you may prefer to catch the bus from Heathfield to avoid road walking. To reach the trig point at Cross-in-Hand you need to leave the main A267 by turning left and following the B2102 Ringmer/Lewes road westwards, this road leaving the A267 opposite a petrol station. Follow the B2102 for a little over a quarter of a mile, passing a minor road turning which is to the right, then just beyond this minor road turning you bear right up the narrow Mill Lane which leads you to the old (now sail-less) windmill. Immediately before the mill to the left is a field, accessed by a gate, in which you will find the trig point; the views from the trig point itself are magnificent especially to the south-west and south-east. Retrace your steps to Cross-in-Hand for buses back to Horam.

East Sussex/Brighton and Hove Walks 21 - 40

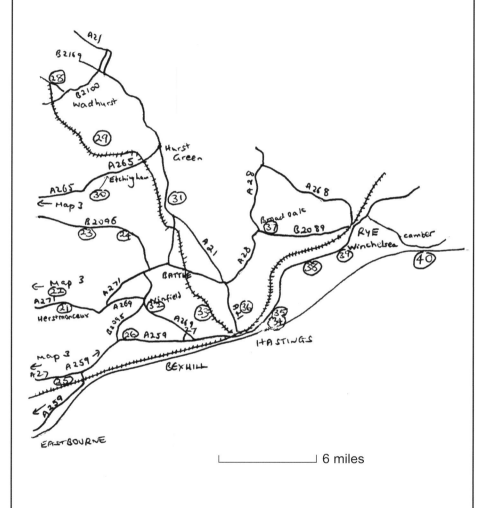

6 miles

21 Windmill Hill/Herstmonceux x 3
TQ647122/644102/645106/651100 EASY.

Regular buses(SC) serving Windmill Hill and Herstmonceux on Eastbourne-Bexhill-Hastings route. 4.5 miles. R Windmill Hill(P,S), Herstmonceux(P,S).

You will pick up a bumper haul of trig points on this walk - four in just over four miles! From the pub by the little green in the centre of Windmill Hill on the A271 between Herstmonceux and Ninfield, walk westwards on the south side of the A271 to the modest embankment on your side of the road, with the splendid white-painted windmill just opposite. Climb the embankment - it's a bit of a scramble, with a lot of vegetation - and negotiate the fence to enter a field, keeping a little substation to your left; the trig point is in the field and commands excellent views across the Pevensey Levels. There is no public right of way into this field, so please refer to my introductory notes. Retrace your steps to the first approach road to the pub at the top of the little green, but rather than turning left to reach the pub go straight on south-westwards down Comphurst Lane with clear signing to Comphurst and a NO CARS warning. Follow Comphurst Lane, going forward on an obvious if narrow path which swings in a more southerly direction in the shade of trees, emerging into open fields, widening and going steeply downhill. As you walk, you can enjoy fine views to Herstmonceux Place to your right. At the foot of the hill the path becomes a clearer mud track which crosses a stream and swings to the right; as it does so, turn left onto a path that heads clearly across a field,

One of the harder trig points to access - the Windmill Hill trig point

A sunlit trig point at Herstmonceux....

A capped trig point at Herstmonceux.....

southwards and uphill. You enter a wood and follow the obvious path southwards then just west of south through the wood, shortly arriving at a footpath crossroads+. Turn left here to follow a clear path south-eastwards, soon emerging from the wood and entering a field; bear left here* and follow the field edge round to the very top right-hand corner, exiting the field by the gate** and turning left onto a tarmac drive. Follow the drive briefly, then take the first left turn up a driveway where at the time of writing there were various pieces of farm paraphernalia, and you will see the first of the three Herstmonceux trig points on the green. Return to the gate double-asterisked, pass through it and now bear left to walk

And one more at Herstmonceux!

through the centre of the field to be reunited with and turn left onto the path from which you departed at the single-asterisked point above. Go forward to cross over another drive as signposted, and continue on the clear path through a pleasant wooded area with Herstmonceux Castle to the left; the path emerges from the wooded area and goes straight ahead across the meadow, with beautiful views to the castle and the old observatory, now a science centre. Soon you reach a crossroads*** of paths, and here turn left to follow the clearly defined 1066 Country Walk, continuing along this path and going through a gate, then begin to climb gently uphill. You pass a very narrow clearing in the trees to your right, then as thicker woodland starts on your right, look to your left at the large green domes of the observatory; just before you get level with the first, bear right on what is the first path leading off into the woods and follow it through the woods, the woodland soon opening out on the right. You reach a path fork, with a rougher path going off to the right, and here you take the left path which immediately arrives at a lawn with the second Herstmonceux trig point neatly placed in the centre and another impressive dome to the left. Retrace your steps to the crossroads triple-asterisked above and this time continue along the 1066 Country Walk through the trees to arrive shortly at a tarmac drive; turn right and very soon you'll see the third and last Herstmonceux trig point on a little green, with an almost surreal backcloth of what can only be described as futuristic buildings. This trig point is now used as part of the Ordnance Survey's GPS system. Return to the track and bear right, follow the track briefly to arrive at the bottom end of a metalled road, then turn right to follow it, with Herstmonceux Church to your left. Now you have a choice. To return to Windmill Hill you need to follow the road very briefly then turn right onto a clearly signed path which enters the woods and soon arrives back at the footpath crossroads marked + above. Just retrace your steps from there to Windmill Hill. Alternatively, for variety you could proceed from here to the centre of "new" Herstmonceux (which provides the start of the Bodle Street Green trig point walk described below in walk 22), and to do this you need to walk a full mile up the road via Flowers Green to Chapel Row; virtually opposite the old chapel, just beyond Lime Walk, turn left onto a signed footpath which climbs through a pleasant grassy area giving good views across to Windmill Hill then descends along a metalled path to reach the A271 and the modern centre of Herstmonceux. There are plenty of amenities here including good bus connections back to Windmill Hill or further afield to Eastbourne, Bexhill and Hastings.

22 Bodle Street Green TQ641164 MODERATE.

Regular buses(SC) serving Hailsham and Herstmonceux on Eastbourne-Bexhill-Hastings route. 12 miles maximum, 6 miles minimum. R Herstmonceux(P,S), Cowbeech(P), Hailsham(P,C,S).

This trig point will test the dedication of the trig point explorer in the sense that it is very disappointingly sited and a long way from public transport links. However this walk - which could very easily be coupled with walk 21 above - incorporates some charming riverside walking and a section of disused railway and there is an "escape route" if 12 miles is too much. Start in the modern centre of Herstmonceux, which sits astride the A271, by making for West End, the road for Cowbeech, heading north-westwards away from the main village street. However, having joined West End turn almost immediately right into the metalled Bagham Lane and follow it to just short of the buildings of the farms of Wenhurst and Nunningham. A footpath sign directs you round the left side of the buildings beyond which you proceed north-eastwards, a signpost directing you initially, and follow the stiles through the fields; the path is indistinct, and you should avoid being tempted along a track that runs initially parallel with your route then disappears to the right. Continuing to aim for the stiles and heading north-eastwards, pass directly under the pylons and descend, crossing over a small footbridge then, once on the valley bottom, making for a more substantial footbridge over Pebsham Stream. Cross the footbridge, bear left and continue along the obvious marked path which keeps the stream to the left, firstly through woodland then meadows. In due course you arrive at the metalled Chilsham Lane onto which you turn right and which you follow uphill to a T-junction; turn left and follow the road - linking Bodle Street Green with Rushlake Green - for about three quarters of a mile, bending sharply left at Red House Farm and more gently right at Thorneyfold Farm. Soon after this right bend there's a left-hand turning with Thorneyfold Cottage just opposite. Don't take the left turning, but just past it turn left onto a signed footpath which goes up a steep bank to a field; bear half right and cross the field, aiming for a gate which you cross to enter another field, and keeping to the right-hand field boundary and aiming to the right of a pig shed, go forward to cross a metalled drive with farm buildings to your left. Climb up the metalled slipway, passing the farm paraphernalia. Ignoring gates to your left, go straight ahead to a gate and enter a field, following the left-hand field edge to discover the trig point coyly tucked in the hedge on the left, but please note that there is no public right of way across the field and you should refer to my introductory notes. There are sadly no views to speak of. You could just retrace your steps to Herstmonceux if you wished, but to continue, go on to the corner of the field, bearing left to cross into the adjacent field, then immediately right along the right-hand field edge with a tree-shaded pond to your right. Go forward into a wider field and descend steeply, following a line just to the right of the buildings of Iwood Place Farm that are on the hillside above and ahead, and aiming for a stile. Enter the woodland by means of the stile and join a path that veers almost immediately left and proceeds pleasantly through the wood, although it's a bit indistinct in places. You're joined by a fence just to your left - there's a pond below to the left and views through the trees to fields to your right - and you go forward to emerge at a T-junction with a wider farm track, turning left to follow the track downhill then uphill a little. You'll shortly come to a gate on your left which leads into a field going uphill, and you need to go through the gate and rise through the field, keeping the boundary to your right; continue in the same direction, crossing what looks like a newly-made farm track, and arrive at a road with the beautiful Iwood Place farmhouse straight ahead. Turn left to follow the road very briefly past the Iwood Place Farm complex. Just beyond the farm, turn right onto a plinth-signed path at first going parallel with the road then striking out just west of south, aiming for the right side of woods ahead. Head for and cross the stile then turn right onto a farm lane which soon swings left to reach the splendid timber-framed Batsford Farm House, bearing to the right of the house and reaching a stile, then going left along the left-hand edge of the field, aiming for a gate. Pass through it and descend south-westwards, aiming for thick woodland and a line of pylons ahead of you; as you reach the valley bottom, aim for the footbridge and cross it, directly under the pylons, then use the steps to climb up through the charming Clippenham Woods to emerge at a field. Go forward through the field in the same direction, heading for the Clippenham Farm buildings, then join a track through the farm and continue along it to reach the road. Turn left and follow the road to Cowbeech with its welcome pub. From the pub you could continue along the road then shortly turn left along a road which in less than a mile and a half brings you back to

Herstmonceux. Alternatively, just beyond the pub turn right onto the road signposted Warbleton and follow it for just under half a mile to immediately beyond the Blackford Farm turning but before the rather ugly waterworks! Just beyond the Blackford Farm turning, bear left through a stile onto a signed path through overgrown meadows, keeping the Cuckmere River to your right; you cross a footbridge and veer north-west, with the Cuckmere River close by to your left. The river, and your parallel path, veers westwards, passing to the south of Knightsbridge Farm to arrive at a road crossing. Cross the road and bear right, almost immediately arriving at a signed path onto which you turn left and which you now follow fractionally north of west, the river to your left. Soon you swing south-westwards and it's now lovely easy walking through the meadows, with the old Polegate-Tunbridge Wells railway to your right. Look out for a stone overbridge across the railway; work your way to the left of this to reach a grassy track which is carried by the overbridge, follow the track over the bridge, then walk westwards to arrive shortly at a footpath crossroads. Turn left and head south-westwards, keeping a hedge to the right, then pass a pond which is to your right and swing more obviously southwards to reach a T-junction with a road. Bear left and follow the road past a weir and crossing of the Cuckmere, soon reaching a slipway, then turn right up the slipway to join the old railway. Now follow the old line - the Cuckoo Trail - which is clearly signposted all the way to Hailsham, passing the magnificently preserved old Hellingly railway station building en route; there are excellent bus connections from Hailsham back to Herstmonceux and further afield to Eastbourne, Bexhill and Hastings.

23 Woods Corner TQ709195 EASY.
Infrequent buses(ESCC) serving Woods Corner on Heathfield-Battle route. 1 mile. R Woods Corner(P).

This walk works well as a pub stroll from the Swan pub, Woods Corner, the crossroads junction of the B2096 Heathfield-Battle road and the Burwash-Herstmonceux road. From the Swan head eastwards alongside the B2096, and in a couple of hundred yards you will see a narrow path signed SUGAR LOAF going off to the left; follow this, heading for the Sugar Loaf monument, one of the follies of "Mad Jack" Fuller, the trig point situated immediately beside the path on the left a little way before the monument. The views from here are disappointing but the monument is well worth seeing. Beyond the monument continue northwards over the field then at the bottom turn right to follow the left-hand field edge, keeping woodland to your left and enjoying superb views to the north-east while you walk. As the woodland to the left relents, look half right to the buildings marked on OS maps as Christmas Farm; use a stile to turn right into the field just west of the farm, and walk across the field to return to the B2096 beside the buildings, savouring further tremendous views, this time to the south. Bear right to follow the B2096 back to the Swan.

24 Netherfield TQ709195 MODERATE.

Infrequent buses(ESCC) serving Netherfield on Heathfield-Battle route. 1 mile. R Netherfield(P,S).

NOTE: THIS TRIG POINT IS IN THE MIDDLE OF A CORN FIELD. YOU SHOULD THEREFORE AVOID DOING THIS WALK DURING CORN-GROWING TIME. The walk starts at the White Hart pub on the B2096 Heathfield-Battle road at Netherfield. Walk westwards beside this road to the far west end of the village, turning right to follow a farm lane signed Darwell Beech, but noting that a signpost at a gate along this lane tells you that unauthorised access is prohibited - refer to my introductory notes. Continue along the lane beyond the gate, the lane soon swinging sharply right; as it does so, bear left and walk gently uphill alongside a field boundary to the south-west edge of an area of woodland. Bear right here and follow the left-hand field edge keeping the trees to your left. When you reach a sharp left bend, the ground ahead starts to slope down; don't bear left downhill but leave the field edge, walk straight ahead and you will reach the trig point at the highest point of the corn field, enjoying fantastic views to the Weald and the coast. Retrace your steps to the White Hart for well-earned refreshment!

The Netherfield trig point on a glorious Wealden summer morning

25 Stone Cross TQ618046 EASY.
Regular buses(EB) serving Stone Cross from Eastbourne. 1 mile. R Stone Cross(P,S).

The walk starts from the Stone Cross village church at the junction of Hailsham Road and Dittons Road. Head eastwards from the traffic lights along Rattle Road, noting the windmill on the right; a couple of hundred yards beyond the mill, at the Inglenook Cattery sign, turn left along a footpath and follow it, kinking left at the end to turn left into Peelings Lane parallel with the A27 bypass. The lane rises gently and as it levels out, you'll see a field to your right separating your lane from the bypass. The trig point is in the middle of the field, and you can only access the field by negotiating a fence, there being no public right of way into the field (please refer to introductory notes), but if you get there you will enjoy good views westwards to the South Downs escarpment. Continue along the lane downhill to arrive back at the church.

The South Downs form a lovely backdrop to the trig point here at Stone Cross

26 Barnhorn TQ692079 MODERATE.
Regular buses(SC) serving Barnhorn on Hastings-Pevensey-Eastbourne route. 3 miles. R none.

The walk starts from the bus stop at the junction of the main A259 with Coneyburrow Road, Barnhorn a little west of Little Common on the outskirts of Bexhill. From the

Cushioned by the grass - the Barnhorn trig point

bus stop, follow the north side of the A259 westwards for a few hundred yards then as the main road bends to the right (at the same time that a minor road goes off it to the left) you reach the buildings of Hill Farm. Turn right here onto the farm road, going gently uphill, then pass through a gate and continue along the farm road, bending sharply right; soon, just beyond the farm buildings, you'll see the trig point to your left, very clearly visible and affording excellent views to the sea and northwards as well. You could just return to the bus stop but for a longer, most enjoyable, walk to the church at Hooe, return to the farm lane and follow it as it heads first north-east then swings north-westwards and descends quite steeply to the valley floor. Having hit the valley bottom, turn left and follow the left-hand field edge round, passing an area of water with copious warning signs and then continuing on an obvious path heading in a generally northerly direction. You soon arrive at a narrow gate which you pass through and proceed along a very narrow path indeed; you then swing just south of west but almost immediately then bear right up the hill towards the houses on the hilltop. Follow the path to the houses and the road, and cross over the road to join another, minor road which you follow past more houses on the right* heading north-westwards. The road bends sharply left; as it does so, bear right and head north-eastwards along a track which becomes a path and takes you to the delightful church of St Oswald, Hooe. Having inspected the church, retrace your steps through the churchyard and on exiting from it you bear left to follow the the left-hand edge of the adjacent field just south of east, passing a field boundary. At the next field boundary there is a signed right turn, but note that the turn is just before, not beyond, the boundary hedge; bear right here and follow the left-hand field edge downhill, then go up the other side to arrive at the houses asterisked above. Turn left onto the road and retrace your steps to the start.

27 The Mount, Bexhill TQ749092 MODERATE.
Regular buses(SC) serving Sidley on Eastbourne-Bexhill-Hastings route. 1.5 miles. R Sidley(P,S).

Your walk starts at the junction of the A269 London Road and the A2036 Wrestwood Road at the south-east end of Sidley in the outskirts of Bexhill. Follow the A269 north-westwards from here towards the centre of Sidley, very shortly turning right into Bank Road and going forward into a twitten which emerges in Meadow Crescent; carry straight on along Meadow Crescent which swings left to reach Glovers Lane. Turn right into Glovers Lane and follow it as far as the footbridge over the old Crowhurst-Bexhill railway, enjoying lovely views northwards from just short of the bridge. Cross the

The Mount, Bexhill trig point with reservoir accompaniment

footbridge and pass the gate which is on the right, bearing immediately right beyond the gate onto a path that runs between electric fences then swings left* and continues along a left-hand field edge. Follow the obvious path uphill until it swings sharply left. You now need to bear right, underneath the fence, which is not a public right of way(please refer to introductory notes); looking left, up the hill, you'll see a mast, and you now aim for this, going uphill and over a wooden enclosure fence to arrive at the Mount reservoir with the trig point on top. The views aren't brilliant but they are better a little further down. Retrace your steps to the point asterisked above; there's a gap in the fence here which allows you to bear left into the field and join a path which follows the right-hand field edge, going parallel with the old railway which is to your right, then narrowly between the top of the cutting and modern housing to your left. It becomes a concrete path which arrives back at the start point.

28 Best Beech Hill, near Wadhurst TQ620315(2 trig points) EASY.
Regular trains (OPERATED BY SOUTH-EASTERN TRAINS) serving Wadhurst on Tunbridge Wells-Hastings line. 4.5 miles maximum, 2.5 miles minimum. R Wadhurst(P,C,S).

This is a particularly difficult trig point to link conveniently with local public transport by footpaths so most of the walking is along country roads. Turn left out of Wadhurst station car park along the B2099, then take the first left road turn, Faircrouch Lane, in just over half a mile passing Tapsell's Lane. Continue beyond this junction, still on Faircrouch Lane, which swings gently from south-east to south-west; as it bends more sharply right (south-westwards) and becomes Fairglen Road, you leave the road and join a path - shown on maps as a continuation of Faircrouch Lane - which proceeds just west of south uphill through the trees. Shortly you reach a path going hard left off the lane, with a choice of either a traditional path or steps going uphill. At the top there's a fork with the left path going forward to a very attractive viewpoint, while the right path goes to a gate beyond which is a raised grassy area containing TWIN trig points - the only example in Sussex. There's no right of way through the gates, so please refer to my introductory notes. You could now retrace your steps to Wadhurst station, but to vary things en route you could turn right into Tapsell's Lane; just before the house Hathers in a few hundred yards there's a signed path left, shown on maps as the Sussex Border Path that you could follow to Station Road onto which you turn left to return to the station. As a further alternative you could continue along Tapsell's Lane to reach the B2099 at Durgates, turning right here and following the B2099 for just over half a mile to reach and explore the very attractive village of Wadhurst. It's then a mile and a half walk back along the B2099 to the station.

29 Stonegate/Bines Farm TQ674286/644258 MODERATE.
Regular trains(OPERATED BY SOUTH-EASTERN TRAINS) serving Stonegate on Tunbridge Wells-Hastings line. 6 miles. R none.

Here are two walks for the price of one, one all on roads, the other incorporating some pleasant riverside footpaths, but both based at Stonegate station. To begin the first walk, turn right out of the station approach road onto Peartree Hill and proceed up this road for a mile to Stonegate village; at the crossroads in the village centre, turn right along Cottenden Road which you follow for just under half a mile. Just before the houses of the hamlet of Cottenden on the left-hand side, bear left onto a farm track, follow it gently uphill and you'll soon see the Stonegate trig point on the right from which there are pleasant views, even though the setting of the trig point isn't spectacular. Retrace your steps to the top of the Stonegate station approach road. If you wish to visit the second trig point don't go back down to the station, but rather continue south-westwards along the road down into the East Sussex Rother valley; the road swings more westwards then south-westwards again and shortly, as the road begins to climb, take the first right turn along a minor road for just under half a mile to reach Bines Farm. Turn left at the

5.45am on a July morning - dawn breaks over the Bines Farm trig point

road junction here* and follow the road initially southwards, but almost immediately, as the road swings left (eastwards) bear right onto a signed bridleway which proceeds just east of south, rising gently. Soon a signed footpath goes off to the right, and, just beyond this right turn, bear left off the path into a very large sloping field which at the time of writing was uncultivated and a mass of weeds. Climb up it steeply and at the top you'll see the Bines Farm trig point from which there are magnificent views westwards. Retrace your steps to the junction asterisked above, but this time bear left onto the road and follow it, passing Waterloo Farm and crossing a bridge over the river Rother. Turn right onto the signed footpath very soon after the bridge crossing, avoiding the more tempting bridleway a little further on, and follow the path north-eastwards along a right-hand field edge. Keep along the path to the corner of the field, then turn hard left and follow the field edge up as far as a stile and a footpath sign which takes you into another field with Bivelham Forge Farm immediately to the left. Continue across the field, heading initially just south of east, with thick woodland to the left and the Rother coming in from the right; the path is indistinct but you won't go wrong if you keep the Rother to your right. Veering north-eastwards, you cross a couple of bridges over tributary streams then go forward to a very well-defined path through a crop field, at the end of which you go over two more bridges in close succession, with the very prominent Witherenden Farm buildings immediately ahead of you. Now veering eastwards, take the path uphill towards the farm but about halfway up the hill turn right onto a signed path through a field, and follow it. Keeping the farm buildings close by to your left, aim for the left-hand side of another farm which soon comes into view straight ahead, exit the field by a clearly signed path, and go forward to a T-junction with a metalled lane. Turn right and follow the lane to a T-junction with a road, here turning left and soon arriving back at Stonegate station.

30 Socknersh Manor TQ698235 MODERATE.

Infrequent buses(ESCC) serving Burwash on Heathfield-Etchingham route; regular trains(OPERATED BY SOUTH-EASTERN TRAINS) serving Etchingham on Tunbridge Wells-Hastings line. 6 miles. R Burwash(P,C,S), Etchingham(P,S).

Your walk starts at the church towards the eastern end of the main street of the pretty village of Burwash. Proceed to the east end of the churchyard to join a footpath which heads eastwards and continues along the hilltop, with superb views down to the Dudwell valley. You pass through a gate and enter another field, maintaining height; passing to the right of a strip of woodland, with a gate leading into it, you enter a further field with corrugated iron farm buildings to your left. Walk diagonally right across this field, aiming for and walking through a gap into another field, heading downhill, then proceed through another gap into a further field, following a rather indistinct green strip south-eastwards through this field to a footbridge over a ditch in the trees. The signposting, wholly inadequate thus far, now improves; follow the footpath arrows to continue round the right-hand side of an area of woodland and then proceed, still south-eastwards, downhill towards the valley floor. Go forward to a footbridge over the river Dudwell and proceed as signposted just south of east, rising, passing through a gate and dropping down to a signed junction with a bridleway* . Turn right to follow the bridleway as signed, soon joining a metalled driveway and proceeding southwards to a T-junction with Fontridge Lane. Bear right onto the lane and follow it for a few hundred yards to a left turn signposted Socknersh Manor. Follow the Socknersh Manor road until it shortly swings right; here go off the drive to the left, climbing the bank and following

Woodland retreat - the Socknersh Manor trig point

the field boundary, soon reaching the trig point in a clearing in the hedge. Views are limited but the surroundings are beautifully unspoilt. Return to Fontridge Lane, turn right and, if you're pushed for time, follow the lane for a mile to a T-junction and turn left to reach Etchingham. However a prettier route is as follows: return to the point asterisked above but this time continue along the signed bridleway and follow the footpath signs round the buildings of Grandturzel, the way very obvious between the electric fences. Signs direct you to a footbridge back over the Dudwell, and from this footbridge you continue as signposted, northwards, to a field boundary, then veer north-eastwards, aiming for a cluster of buildings making up the Borders Farm complex. Pass to the right of a large pond/gravel pit then swing in a more easterly direction and aim to the right of the Borders buildings; cross over a very decrepit stile and footbridge, follow the footpath signs left through the farm complex to arrive at a metalled minor road, and turn right onto the road which you follow into Etchingham. The station is off the main road at the east end of the village.

31 Hooks Beech/Battle TQ767209/TQ747165 MODERATE, STRENUOUS IN PLACES.

Regular trains (OPERATED BY SOUTH-EASTERN TRAINS) serving Robertsbridge and Battle on Tunbridge Wells-Hastings line. 7 miles. R Robertsbridge(P,C,S), Battle(P,C,S).

The walk starts at Robertsbridge station. Bear right out of the station building, turning left into Station Road and following it just north of east to a T-junction with the High Street. Turn left into the High Street then very shortly bear right into Fair Lane and follow it to its end. When you get to the end, bear right to use a footbridge across the busy A21; having crossed, you need to turn right along a signed footpath which initially runs parallel with the A21 southwards then strikes out just north of east through trees, arriving at the corner of a field. Veering south-eastwards now, walk downhill through the middle of the field, the course of the path very obvious, aiming for a footbridge and sewage works ahead. Cross the bridge and walk gently uphill past the sewage works to the edge of a wood; don't cross the stile but take the path to the left of the stile which goes due east through the woods in a straight line. You reach the east end of the wood and having emerged, veer right as directed and follow a path along the right-hand field edge, keeping the woods immediately to the right. At one point a signpost seems to direct you into the wood, but stay just to the left of it and reach a path junction with a wider track coming in from the left and going straight ahead; follow the track that does go straight on, passing Keepers Cottages and descending to a gate and an insulated electric fence crossing. Go straight over both and, keeping in the same direction(just

west of south) go steeply uphill and forward to Poppinghole Lane, bearing left onto the lane and following it all the way to the T-junction with the B2089 at Swaile's Green, a distance of 2 miles. Turn right to follow the B2089 towards Hooks Beech(note that maps show a footpath short cut from Poppinghole Lane to Hooks Beech but this path has unfortunately been fenced off and is unavailable). Just under half a mile from where you joined the B2089, you come to the hamlet of Hooks Beech and a sharp left bend, indicated by a black and white direction arrow board. There's another similar adjacent board for motorists coming the other way, and it

The Battle trig point, a few minutes' walk from the bustling town centre

is in fact a few yards past this second board that you'll see the Hooks Beech trig point sitting in the hedge. If you want to get a bit closer to it, backtrack to the stile (signifying the public footpath that's now no more!) cross it and bear immediately left alongside the hedge to inspect it; it now has an impressive ivy coating but it has clearly seen better days! Return to the B2089 and follow it on south-westwards through Vinehall Forest, and when, on emerging from the forest, the road forks, take the left fork and shortly arrive at a T-junction with the A21. Turn left to follow briefly beside this very busy road - there's no pavement, so take care - then in a couple of hundred yards, turn right down the Maddomswood Farm road, a plinth-signed public right of way. Keep along the metalled road downhill south-westwards, then as the road veers sharply right, leave it and go through the gate onto an unsigned and not very clear path which heads, in the same south-westerly direction, down to the valley floor and into the trees to the bank of a stream. Turn left to follow the bank for a few yards and arrive at a footbridge; bear right to cross the footbridge and reach a path junction with signed paths right, left and ahead! Go straight ahead through the meadow, veering left and rising slightly, aiming for the top left-hand corner of the meadow and going forward to cross over the railway by means of a bridge. Beyond the bridge crossing go on to a T-junction with a farm lane, here bearing left along the lane to reach the hamlet of Wood's Place. About 20 yards or so before the lane veers sharply left, turn right as if entering the complex of rather rundown buildings, and very soon you'll see a footpath arrow sign which directs you left, under cover, to a stile; cross the stile and now head downhill fractionally west of south through pasture, the path hardly discernible. However on reaching the valley bottom you aim for a very smart new footbridge and clearly signed path beyond, taking you half left, south-eastwards, to another smart stream crossing beyond which you see the path, clearly signposted and well defined, heading just west of south steeply uphill. Follow the path uphill, going forward to a very sturdy stile which you cross, then veering in a more south-westerly direction you continue to follow a clear track through the pasture, now enjoying good views across the Weald and aiming just west of the hilltop Lower Gate Farm in the shade of trees. You cross a second, equally sturdy stile, then bear almost immediately left along the left side of a barn, going forward to arrive shortly at the Lower Gate Farm road; turn left onto the farm road and follow it to a T-junction with Whatlington Road onto which you turn right and which you follow, a pavement soon provided as you enter the outskirts of Battle. You shortly pass Virgin's Lane, a turning to the right, and beyond this turning you rise quite sharply. You then begin the descent into the town, but very shortly after the descent begins you need to look out for, and follow, a plinth-signed footpath/driveway going off to the right; a further visual aid to identify this for you is a brown wooden sign saying KINGS MEAD WINDMILL. Follow the driveway to the end, bearing left to a signed Open Space area where you will see the Battle trig point from which the views are superb, certainly compensating for the non-existent ones at Hooks Beech. You should take a look at the windmill just to the right here; it has undergone a quite astonishing conversion into a private house, with the sails still on it. Retrace your steps to Whatlington Road and turn right to walk down the road - now Caldbec Hill and subsequently becoming Mount Street - into the centre of Battle. (There's no reason, of course, why you couldn't do the Battle trig point as an "out and back" walk from the delightful centre of Battle.) To reach the station you need to turn left from Mount Street into the High Street(A2100) then simply continue along the A2100 south-eastwards via Upper Lake and Lower Lake, bearing left into Station Approach; from the centre of Battle it's a brisk 10/15-minute walk which you probably won't appreciate if you've walked all the way from Robertsbridge.

32 Ninfield TQ700128 EASY.

Regular buses(SC) serving Ninfield on Eastbourne-Bexhill-Hastings route. 1.5 miles. R Ninfield (P,S).

Your walk starts in the centre of Ninfield, at the junction of High Street and Manchester Road. Walk westwards along the High Street until you come to an open area on the right with a very prominent watertower, and you will see the raised grassy platform in this area with the trig point on the top. The area is private but if you can get to the trig point - you should refer to my introductory notes - it is well worth seeing, as the views are excellent and the trig point itself, beautifully maintained, bears a plaque showing that it has been adopted in commemoration of World War 2 Resistance fighters. Return to the High Street, cross over, turn right and then bear very shortly left down Moor Hall Drive. Shortly you'll see a signed footpath leading left, south-

The "adopted" trig point at Ninfield

eastwards, off the drive; follow the signed path across the fields, crossing a field boundary and walking downhill along a left-hand field edge. As you approach the hill bottom, bear left onto a signed footpath heading north-east and soon entering an area of woodland, known as Church Wood. This is a delightful area of woodland, very user-friendly for walkers. Keep to the left of the pond and go over the new, very smart, footbridge, continuing along the obvious path and veering gradually eastwards and then just south of east to exit the wood and make your way uphill towards the church. Just before the church bear left onto a clear path northwards, enjoying really lovely views towards the sea, and you will emerge at the High Street where you began.

33 Swineham Lane, Crowhurst TQ766117 MODERATE.
Regular trains (OPERATED BY SOUTH-EASTERN TRAINS)serving Crowhurst on Tunbridge Wells-Hastings line. 2.5 miles. R Crowhurst(S).

From Crowhurst station walk down Station Road south-westwards, bearing left along the main street, then at the fork junction bear left into Chapel Hill, following this road as it proceeds south-eastwards past the chapel and bends sharply left. Shortly the road, now Sandrock Hill, swings sharply right, and you'll see that on the bend there is to the left a housing development and a small car park for residents and their visitors. Just before this car park turn left as indicated by a path sign onto a lane which proceeds past houses then continues north-eastwards; continue to a sign which warns you that there is no path beyond, and here* turn right off the lane onto a very narrow path which immediately crosses over the old Crowhurst-Bexhill railway. You arrive at a gully and here bear right along a narrow path on the right-hand side of the gully in the shade of trees, climbing steadily. You reach a gate with a field beyond, but just before the gate bear left to continue on a very narrow often overgrown and potentially very muddy path uphill through quite thick vegetation. The path emerges at Swineham Lane. Turn right and almost immediately pass the entrance to a riding school; beyond the entrance there is a hedge running parallel with the road on the right, and the trig point is hidden in the hedge. On no account should you trespass into the riding school grounds, tempting though it may be to try and obtain better views. Retrace your steps to the point asterisked above, but this time go straight over the lane onto an obvious signed path through fields, proceeding north-westwards and aiming for Crowhurst church which you passed at the start. You descend to a footbridge and, ignoring a path going off to the left here, cross the bridge and continue to aim for the church. Shortly you arrive at the road onto which you turn right and which you follow, then, by the church, bear right again up Station Road to return to Crowhurst station.

34 East Hill, Hastings TQ833101 STRENUOUS.
Regular trains to Hastings from Brighton, Eastbourne, Ashford and London. 2 miles. R Hastings(P,C,S).

From the road end of the pier on the front at Hastings, walk eastwards along the seafront past the various seaside amusement areas, until the main road swings sharply away to the left; where it does this, continue walking along Rock-a-Nore Road but look out carefully for the Tamarisk Steps which go off to the left a few yards into Rock-a-Nore Road. Climb the steps to the top, then at the top of the steps bear left into Tackleway. Very shortly, however, bear right to climb further steps* onto East Hill, going forward onto the clifftops; follow the grassy cliff path which maintains a reasonably level course until in a few hundred yards you reach an area of woodland and a choice between bearing slightly right and losing height, or bearing left, parallel with the woods. You do in fact need to take the latter option, gaining height a little and going forward to a smart information board, just before which you'll see a track going off to the right, into the woods. Turn right to follow the track briefly. As soon as you enter the trees, the track begins to descend and a fence starts on the right; immediately opposite, to the left of the track, there's a very steep wooded bank which you need to climb. There is a very narrow way through the thick vegetation but it is a hands-and-knees job! Keep climbing,

Use of hands and knees necessary to access this trig point at East Hill, Hastings

bearing a little left, and you'll see the trig point at the top of the bank nestling in the vegetation; it's unlikely you'll be able to stand to view it, and you'll probably have to crawl up to it. Sadly the views are non-existent, although if the surrounding vegetation could be cleared, they would potentially be superb. Having clambered back down the bank, you could just return the way you came, but you might opt for one of a number of routes back across East Hill to reach the top of the steps asterisked above; the building at the top of the (at the time of writing non-operational) funicular railway is immediately behind the steps and provides a useful marker. Now it just remains for you to drop back down into Hastings and its wide range of amenities.

35 North Seat, Ore TQ843119 MODERATE.
Regular buses(SC) serving Ore from Hastings. 1 mile. R Ore(P,S).

Your walk starts from the junction of the A259 with Fairlight Road, Ore, a mile and a half north-east of the seafront at Hastings. Head east along Fairlight Road then in just over a quarter of a mile bear left into Beacon Road, heading north-eastwards; the road becomes a path and climbs quite steeply, arriving at a viewpoint and topograph with magnificent views. You'll see the trig point a short way beyond the topograph to the left of the path. From here, you could just retrace your steps to the start, but since the trig point is situated in Hastings Country Park with its wealth of paths and open spaces you may wish to explore the park with its beautiful views and variety of plants and wildlife before you return.

36 Baldslow TQ799129 EASY.
Regular buses(SC) serving top of Harrow Lane, Baldslow from Hastings. 0.5 miles. R Baldslow(S).

The walk starts at the top (northern) end of Harrow Lane at its junction with The Ridge at Baldslow in the outskirts of Hastings; there's a bus stop just outside the shop on the east side of Harrow Lane very close to its meeting with The Ridge. From this bus stop walk very briefly southwards along Harrow Lane to a crossroads with paths going right and left. Take the path going left and walk gently uphill, soon reaching an open field which is to the right; the trig point is in the field, close to the path, and there are excellent views towards the coast. You could retrace your steps here, or walk a little further up the path then bear left into a field and follow the right-hand field edge all the way round to obtain fine views across the East Sussex countryside. Return to the original path and retrace your steps to the bus stop.

37 Blackland Wood TQ851212 MODERATE.
Regular buses(ESCC) serving Broad Oak on Hastings-Tenterden route. 5 miles. R Broad Oak(P,S).

From the centre of Broad Oak village, follow the A28 northwards, dropping quite steeply to reach the crossing of the river Tillingham at Arnold Bridge about half a mile from Broad Oak. Cross the bridge and immediately bear right onto a driveway, keeping the river to your right. As the driveway veers to the left, join a signed path which crosses the river and keeps it to the left; shortly you're signposted back onto the other side and you now keep the river to your right, soon entering Furnace Wood. Your path passes through the trees and emerges to follow a field edge with fencing to your left and the river immediately to your right. You arrive at a crossing of Furnace Lane, with Furnace Farm just opposite; turn right to cross the river then straightaway bear left along a signed track which keeps farm buildings to the left, while within view to the right is a fine oast house. Just beyond the buildings, the path divides, and you take the left fork, soon arriving back beside the river. You can now enjoy a lovely walk beside the river through delightful meadow scenery, keeping the river to your left and going forward to arrive at another metalled road at Hundredhouse Bridge. Turn left to follow the road, Hundredhouse Lane, passing Ludley Farm and, ignoring a road going off to the right,

walking steeply uphill; you enter woodland and pass another road going off to the right, then shortly bear left into Moore's Lane, heading now just south of west and continuing through the woods. Shortly before the road bends slightly right, bear right onto a forest track signed Blackland Wood. Follow this track briefly, and, looking out very carefully to your left, you will see the trig point nestling in a tiny clearing amongst the trees; there is no path access so to get to it so you'll have to struggle through the undergrowth! Sadly the views are negligible but the trig point is well maintained and the surroundings are very peaceful. To return to Broad Oak you could just return to Moore's Lane, follow it in a north-westerly then westerly

White on green - the trig point at Blackland Wood

direction to a T-junction with Furnace Lane, turn left onto this lane and follow it back to the A28 at Broad Oak, turning left to return to the village centre. Alternatively on reaching Furnace Farm, reached very soon after joining Furnace Lane, you could retrace your steps alongside the Tillingham back to Arnold Bridge and then beside the A28 back to the centre of Broad Oak.

38 Icklesham TQ874165 EASY.

Regular buses(SC) serving Icklesham on Folkestone-Lydd-Rye-Hastings route. 1 mile. R Icklesham(P).

This trig point is in the back garden of 2 High Fords Close. As such it is out of bounds and viewable only by appointment with the owners. PLEASE DO NOT ATTEMPT TO TRESPASS ONTO THIS PROPERTY. IF YOU WISH TO VIEW IT YOU MUST MAKE AN APPOINTMENT WITH THE OWNERS. From the Robin Hood pub at the western end of Icklesham on the A259 Hastings-Winchelsea road, walk eastwards alongside the main road, turn left into Goldhurst Green and bear right into High Fords, following signs for the School. High Fords Close is the left turning just before the school at the top of the rise. For an attractive walk round the edge of the village, walk back down High Fords, turn right into Goldhurst Green and swing left into Brede Valley View; take the first right turn, bear shortly right at the T-junction and at the end of this

The trig point at Icklesham - only viewable by walking through a private house!

cul-de-sac take the path going forward from here (slightly to the right of the end of the road). Follow this path round the northern edge of the village, enjoying good views to the river Brede valley, going forward onto a lane and passing the pretty and popular Queen's Head Inn. Continue on into Parsonage Lane, then at its end bear right onto the A259 and follow it back to the Robin Hood. If you wanted to detour to the church en route you'd need to cross over the A259 at the end of Parsonage Lane into Workhouse Lane, soon turning left onto a signed path and proceeding to the church.

39 Winchelsea TQ901175 EASY.
Regular buses(SC) serving Winchelsea on Folkestone-Lydd-Rye-Hastings route. 1 mile. R Winchelsea(P,C,S).

Your walk starts from the New Inn in the beautiful old town of Winchelsea. From the front of the pub, turn left then at the crossroads - effectively the centre of the town, with the village sign just to your right here - turn left again and walk briefly westwards past the side of the pub to reach the main A259. Cross with care to a gate. Beyond the

gate is a field and looking just north of west you'll see the beautifully clean white trig point just to the right of an old beacon; walk briefly northwards alongside the A259 then bear first left along a lane and through a gate taking you into the field. Go forward to the trig point. The views from here are quite magnificent, incorporating a large section of the very attractive valley of the river Brede. Beyond the trig point veer slightly left, between the trig point and the beacon, and walk steeply downhill to a gate; pass through the gate and walk north-westwards downhill along a charming green path, still enjoying magnificent views. The path veers gently right and reaches a junction. Don't go on downhill to the river, but proceed north-eastwards, contouring the hillside, and continue walking round the hillside (ignoring a path going off to the left) now veering

The Winchelsea trig point, above the beautiful Brede valley

south-eastwards. You pass a waterworks and arrive back at the A259 at a sharp bend; turn right to follow the A259 uphill, then, as it bends right, go straight on under an archway along a quieter road to re-enter the town. Turn first right and follow the road southwards back to the New Inn.

40 Jury's Gap TQ 989181 EASY.
Regular buses(SC) serving Camber on Folkestone-Lydd-Rye-Hastings route. 1.5 miles. R Camber(P,S).

From the centre of Camber follow the main village street south-eastwards until it reaches the sea. When it does so, climb up onto the raised promenade and follow it for just over half a mile, enjoying lovely views out across Broomhill Sands. Watch out for the road, running parallel with the promenade, swinging away from the sea at Jury's Gap; just before it does so you'll see the trig point poking out of the green embankment separating the promenade from the road. There are fine views back across the sands and towards the splendid cliffs around Fairlight in the distance. For variety you could retrace your steps back to Camber along the sands.

The Jury's Gap trig point - the most south-easterly in Sussex and the closest trig point to the sea in Sussex

126

~ PART 3 ~
WALKING THE TRIG POINTS ON THE
SOUTH DOWNS WAY

There are a number of trig points on or extremely close to the South Downs Way, hereafter for convenience referred to as SDW. Several guidebooks to the SDW have been written, including SB Publications' own guide written by David Harrison. This section of my book is intended to complement that guide, identifying the trig points along the SDW, stating how they may be linked by walking sections of that route, and providing information as to the availability of public transport to get you to the relevant section and then back from it afterwards. Whilst of course it would be eminently possible to incorporate SDW trig points into some of the described walks in the West Sussex and East Sussex sections, and/or walk to an SDW trig point from a public transport base and then straight back to it again, there is a real satisfaction in linking the trig points by using parts of the national trail. But, as stated, you will need the separate SB Publications guide for more detailed route notes. All nine sections below qualify for a "STRENUOUS" grading.

Section 1 West Harting to Cocking incorporating trig points at West Harting Down/Beacon Hill/Linch Ball **SU762187/807184/848174.**
Regular buses(CL) serving South Harting and Ditcham near West Harting on Chichester-Petersfield route; regular buses(SC) serving Cocking on Chichester-Midhurst route. 11 miles. R Cocking (P,C,S - just off route).

The start of this walk is the road junction of the B2146 South Harting to Petersfield road with a minor road leading to Old Ditcham just west of Torberry Farm and half a mile or so south of the hamlet of Nursted. It is on the bus route and you will need to ask the driver to drop you here; if s/he can or will not, get off at South Harting and walk for a mile and a half towards Petersfield, reaching the junction which is to your left. There are three forks leading off here, and you need the middle one, following the road south-westwards and then climbing very steeply, negotiating a hairpin bend to meet the SDW (actually its old start/finish point) at Sunwood Farm. From Sunwood Farm head briefly eastwards along the signed SDW then in a couple of hundred yards, as the Way kinks a little right, bear right onto a signed bridleway which heads initially south-west then swings south-east and heads uphill, entering an area of woodland. A little before reaching the brow of the hill, bear right into the woodland on a thin path and head for the highest ground. You will find the West Harting Down trig point among the trees, with excellent views through the trees to attractive countryside around Petersfield. Return to the SDW the same way. Now follow the SDW south-eastwards, crossing the B2146 and shortly afterwards the B2141, passing the Harting Hill car park and heading

The West Harting Down trig point amongst the thick woodland near the Hampshire/Sussex border

The Linch Ball trig point with a magnificent downland backcloth

just north of east across Harting Downs. The SDW then turns very sharp right to pass round the western side of Beacon Hill, but to reach the Beacon Hill trig point you need to go straight on, up the very steep-sided Beacon Hill; the trig point is on the hilltop, and it commands fantastic views on a clear day. Follow the path carefully south-eastwards from the trig point, descending very steeply to rejoin the SDW. Follow the SDW in a generally south-easterly direction via Pen Hill, past Buriton Farm and up into the woodlands of Philliswood Down, veering north-eastwards to pass the Devil's Jumps tumuli, entering further woodland

and now veering south-eastwards, your direction of travel all the way to Cocking. You come out of the woods and pass over Didling Hill, maintaining height; just over a mile after emerging from the woods you'll walk a little below the hillside of Linch Ball which is to your left, and you immediately arrive at a crossroads of paths. Don't turn left onto the marked path here but go hard left through the gate and follow the field edge round to reach the trig point on Linch Ball. The views are as good as, if not better than, those from Beacon Hill. Return to the SDW and descend along it via Cocking Down, passing the car park above Cocking (Cocking Hill car park) and immediately then arriving at the A286, with a useful bus stop by the road at this point.

Section 2 Cocking to Amberley incorporating trig points at Heyshott Down/Glatting Beacon/West Burton **SU900166/966131/997126.**
Regular buses(SC) to Cocking Hill car park on Chichester-Midhurst route; regular trains serving Amberley on Chichester-Horsham line. 12 miles. R Cocking (P,C,S - just off route), Houghton Bridge (C), Amberley (P - just off route).

From the A286 crossing follow the SDW south-eastwards uphill, climbing via Hill Barn and Manorfarm Downs, veering in a more easterly direction and now keeping woodland on your right. Once the woodland to the right is reached and the path has levelled out, you pass two path junctions in very close succession, the second being effectively a bridleway crossroads with bridle routes going off north-eastwards and south-westwards from here. Continue eastwards along the SDW beyond this crossroads until in a few hundred yards, with the fields of Heyshott Down on your left and woods to your right, you reach a further path crossroads. Bear left to follow the footpath heading

The Glatting Beacon trig point dwarfed by 20th century technology

129

The Westburton Hill trig point looking eastwards towards the Arun valley

north-eastwards off the SDW, shortly reaching the Heyshott Down trig point from which there are tremendous views northwards to Midhurst and its surroundings. Return to the SDW and follow it just south of east over Graffham Down, swinging in a more south-easterly direction to pass over Littleton Down and descend to the A285 Chichester-Petworth road at Littleton Farm. Cross more or less straight over and continue along the SDW uphill, your path, with a slight kink very early on, proceeding south-eastwards onto Sutton Down, having regained the height you lost when you descended to the A285. The Way shaves the left-hand edge of the woodland of Burton Down, just beyond which and to your left (north-east) you'll become aware of a patch of wood with radio masts on a hill, marked on maps as Glatting Beacon. Shortly before arriving level with that patch of wood you reach a path crossroads, a green carpet path straight ahead, and at this crossroads you turn left onto a path that goes uphill, passing to the left side of the masts/woodland and reaching a T-junction of paths. Turn right and then shortly right again onto a path that goes through the woods to the masts, with the Glatting Beacon trig point immediately to the left of the masts. Sadly from the trig point there are no views to speak of! Retrace your steps down this path, turning right at the T-junction and walking downhill out of the woods along a clear path which heads south-eastwards to arrive back at the SDW. Bear left to follow the SDW in a generally easterly direction over Bignor Hill, passing the well-known landmark of Toby's Stone then swinging south-eastwards and very sharply north-eastwards, dropping steeply downhill to a multi-path junction. Follow the signed SDW south-eastwards uphill, passing immediately below and to the left of Westburton Hill. Continue until the ground levels out and the fencing ends; just by a point where two wooden fence posts are tied together, turn left on the west side of a field boundary - the boundary itself consisting of some rather stumpy trees - to reach the Westburton Hill trig point on the hill, with superb views to the sea, the Weald and the South Downs escarpment. Return the same way to rejoin the SDW and follow it south-eastwards to cross the A29, then head just north of east and begin your descent to the Arun valley, veering sharply south-eastwards and then north-eastwards to drop down to the valley floor and cross the Arun by a footbridge. The SDW goes forward to arrive at the B2139 about halfway between Amberley station and Amberley village, but for a short cut to the station turn right immediately beyond the footbridge and follow the left bank of the Arun to reach the B2139 at Houghton Bridge. Turn left to follow this road to Amberley station just beyond the railway overbridge on the right.

Section 3 Amberley to Washington incorporating trig points at Rackham Hill/Kithurst Hill **TQ053125/082125.**

Regular trains serving Amberley on Chichester-Horsham line; regular buses(SC) serving Washington on Worthing-Pulborough-Midhurst route. 6.25 miles. R Amberley (P - just off route),Washington (P - just off route).

To rejoin the SDW from Amberley station, turn right out of the station forecourt and follow the B2139 briefly, taking the first right-hand road turning into High Titten, now back on the SDW. (If you've followed the SDW direct from the Arun footbridge crossing referred to in Section 2 above, you'll need, on arrival at the B2139, to bear right then left into High Titten.) The road goes north-eastwards uphill and reaches a T-junction at which you turn right, then shortly after the right turn the SDW bears left, off the road, onto a path heading eastwards steeply uphill. You reach the top of the rise only to find yourself confronted with an even steeper climb that gets you onto the escarpment, and progress then becomes easier. However another stiff albeit shorter climb is soon necessary to bring you onto Rackham Hill, and you'll see the Rackham Hill trig point immediately to the right of the path, with a little footpath available for you to reach it in comfort! The views are magnificent, particularly westwards to the Arun valley and also northwards, with the fine Parham House and Parham Park clearly visible just to the north-east. Now continue just south of east, passing a wooded area and then, on emerging, dropping down onto Springhead Hill but remaining on top of the escarpment. You proceed eastwards to a large car park, watching carefully for where the road comes up from the B2139; head for the point where the road reaches the car park and now

The Rackham Hill trig point which even has its own little access path!

leave the SDW by taking a bridlepath heading almost due east and uphill, keeping the SDW slightly below you to the right. While the SDW takes a more south-easterly course, you continue eastwards along the top of the escarpment, soon hugging woodland which is to your left, and you arrive at the Kithurst Hill trig point. Unfortunately the woodland immediately to the north slightly obscures the views in that direction, but this is still a wonderful spot with excellent views particularly to the east. Proceed a few yards beyond the trig point along the path to reach a junction of paths, here turning right to follow a path just west of south to arrive back at the SDW; here turn left to follow the SDW south-eastwards past the Chantry Post car park and over Sullington Hill, then more eastwards over Barnsfarm Hill and down to the A24 crossing. Buses may be available here, but to enjoy the amenities of nearby Washington - and buses from the village - cross the A24 with care, going forward to a road on the other side and swinging north to follow the road downhill.

Section 4 Washington to Upper Beeding incorporating trig points at

Chanctonbury Ring/Steyning Round Hill **TQ134120/160104.**

Regular buses(SC) serving Washington on Worthing-Pulborough-Midhurst route; regular buses(BH) serving Upper Beeding on Steyning-Shoreham route. 6.75 miles. R Washington (P - just off route).

To continue along the SDW from the A24 crossing, don't follow the road downhill to Washington but almost immediately leave the road, forking right onto a lane which then swings sharp right, going forward to a car park which is popular with SDW walkers. Follow the SDW uphill beyond the car park, veering south-eastwards, climbing steadily and entering an area of woodland, veering just south of west before swinging south-eastwards and arriving at a T-junction of tracks. Now back on top of the Downs, you turn left to follow the SDW north-eastwards, heading for the cluster of trees around the famous Chanctonbury Ring hill fort. In very close succession, but before the trees, you pass a DEFRA information board, a path going to the left up to the Chanctonbury dew pond, and a cattle grid; it's just beyond the cattle grid that you need to turn half left up onto the green rise to your left, and as you climb you will soon see the Chanctonbury Ring trig point from which there are quite stupendous views that on a clear day may extend to Brighton and out to sea as far as the Isle of Wight. Return to the SDW and follow it past the fort south-eastwards for just over 2 miles to a point where you're able to look eastwards to Steyning, and you will reach the trig point on Steyning Round Hill, just a few yards off the SDW to the right and impossible to miss! The views are particularly good from here to the coast as well as to Steyning itself. Beyond the trig point you continue south-eastwards, veering due south to join a road which you follow past Steyning Bowl , drifting just east of south, then bear right over Annington Hill and, proceeding just north of east, drop down towards the Adur valley. You join a track, veering right and then sharp left to arrive at a road onto which you turn right; you now

The Chanctonbury Ring trig point, the Ring itself close by

descend to the valley bottom at the hamlet of Botolphs, going forward to a footpath that brings you to the right bank of the river Adur. Cross the footbridge to arrive at the busy A283 Steyning-Shoreham road just south of Upper Beeding with bus links to both Shoreham and Steyning.

The Steyning Round Hill trig point enjoys a lovely open setting

Section 5 Upper Beeding to Pyecombe incorporating trig points at Truleigh Hill/Devil's Dyke **TQ225108/257108.**

Regular buses(BH) serving Upper Beeding on Steyning-Shoreham route; regular buses(BH) serving Pyecombe on Hassocks-Brighton route. 7 miles. R Devil's Dyke (P), Pyecombe (P).

From the A283 crossing head eastwards then north-eastwards uphill, firstly along a path then along a metalled road, then a wide stony driveway which passes the Truleigh Hill Youth Hostel at Tottington Barn. Beyond the hostel the driveway rises and passes a number of masts that are to the left. Just beyond the fourth and final mast, the SDW passes an adjoining building which is to the left and begins to lose height. Immediately beyond this building there's a gate which at the time of writing was locked but it was possible to squeeze through it. To get within sight of the Truleigh Hill trig point, you need to get through this gate into the field beyond; however there's no right of public access through it or indeed into this field, and you should refer to my introductory notes on this subject. If you decide to go for it and enter the field, you make your way up the hillside, veering gently left and aiming for the mast that is to the right. You will shortly reach a barbed wire fence and see the trig point in the middle of the field beyond this fence. The only way to get to it is by climbing over this fence; again there is no public right of access into the field and again you should refer to my introductory notes on the subject. No other trig point on or adjoining the SDW is so difficult to access, and moreover the views though good are not exceptional. Returning to the SDW the same way and rejoining it, you now veer north-eastwards to the viewpoint on Edburton Hill, beyond which you veer south-east and continue in a predominantly easterly direction along the top of the escarpment above Fulking, now heading for the Devil's Dyke. You can tell you're approaching the Dyke, with its very popular hilltop restaurant, by the number of sightseers and kite-fliers. As you get close to the metalled approach road from Brighton, look to your left and you'll see your magnificent views northwards interrupted by a grassy bank with the Devil's Dyke trig point perched on the top; the views, as you can imagine, are tremendous, but you are unlikely to be on your own, especially at weekends and/or in summer. Having detoured to inspect the trig point, return to the SDW and continue very briefly eastwards to the approach road mentioned above - you may like to detour again to visit the restaurant - then continue eastwards briefly, veering north-eastwards to walk along the right-hand side of that extraordinary phenomenon, Devil's Dyke itself. You descend to the Brighton-Poynings road, crossing it and passing through the picturesque hamlet of Saddlescombe, proceeding eastwards and rising once more onto West Hill, then heading north-eastwards to descend to cross over the A27 and enter the pretty village of Pyecombe. You follow the village street past the church then turn left to arrive at the A273 from which buses are available to Hassocks and Brighton.

Section 6 Pyecombe to Falmer OR Southease station+ incorporating trig

points at Ditchling Beacon/Blackcap/Balmer Down **TQ332131/373125/361107** (+ there are no trig points between the A27 crossing, just under 8.5 miles from Pyecombe, and Southease station. Therefore you may wish to vary this walk by leaving the SDW at Balmer Down and walking south-westwards to Falmer with excellent bus and train links to Brighton and Lewes).
Regular buses(BH) serving Pyecombe on Hassocks-Brighton route; regular trains serving Southease on Brighton-Seaford line; regular trains serving Falmer on Brighton-Lewes line. 15 miles maximum, 8.25 miles minimum. R Pyecombe (P).

From the junction of Pyecombe village street with the A273, bear left and walk briefly northwards beside the busy A273, shortly turning right to proceed eastwards, uphill along a bridlepath, with a golf course to the right. In just over half a mile you reach a crossroads and here turn left, north-westwards, to pass through New Barn Farm, shortly reaching a sharp turn to the south-east with Clayton Windmills a short distance to the north-west. Having turned south-eastwards, proceed uphill to reach the top of the escarpment, now following the top of the downs and enjoying magnificent views which culminate in Ditchling Beacon, the highest point on the SDW, just under 2 miles from

The Blackcap trig point with its beautiful views across the Weald

The Balmer Down trig point just a short way off the SDW near Falmer

the windmills. The Ditchling Beacon trig point is easily found just to the right of the SDW, and on a decent day, as at Devil's Dyke, you will certainly not be alone! You pass the car park and cross the road with care - for a minor road, it can be very busy - then continue along the top of the escarpment, predominantly just south of east, via Western Brow and Plumpton Plain above Plumpton village. You then reach a multi-path junction where there is a sharp turn of the SDW to the right (south-west).* However, you need to leave the SDW briefly here to locate the trig point at Blackcap, so go straight over the junction then shortly veer left onto the path that stays on top of the escarpment, soon reaching the Blackcap trig point. The views southwards to the Downs, Ouse valley and the sea are excellent, and there are good views to the Weald as well, although there is a patch of woodland immediately behind the trig point blocking northward views straight ahead. Return to the junction asterisked above and now follow the SDW south-westwards for roughly half a mile. Here the SDW turns sharply south-eastwards, but to reach the Balmer Down trig point, continue south-westwards on a white chalk track; you initially descend then rise to a hilltop, and in half a mile or so from the point you left the SDW, you'll see the Balmer Down trig point situated just across the field to the right, and from which the views are fantastic, including the centre of Brighton, Seaford Head and the South Downs escarpment. Now it's decision time. To exercise Option 1 from the trig point (following the SDW all the way to Southease), return to the SDW and follow it south-eastwards over Balmer Down for roughly a mile, then veer south-westwards, round the western edge of Bunkershill Plantation, arriving at the A27 at Housedean Farm. You cross the A27 by means of a bridge, then follow parallel with the A27 eastwards briefly, turning south-westwards here and passing under the railway. You climb to the Newmarket Plantation, veer sharply left to follow the so-called Juggs Road north-eastwards, then proceed south-eastwards over Swanborough Hill, Iford Hill, Front Hill and Mill Hill, veering north-eastwards and descending steeply into the Ouse valley to pass below Rodmell through Southease and eastwards over the Ouse to Southease station. To go for Option 2 from the trig point, a much shorter walk to Falmer, backtrack briefly from the Balmer Down trig point but only as far as a crossroads of paths just a couple of hundred yards downhill, and turn hard left to follow a bridlepath south-westwards; follow the obvious path which swings in a more southerly direction and goes forward to become a metalled road at Ridge Farm. Now follow the metalled road, Ridge Road, in roughly half a mile turning right into Mill Street which you follow to a mini-roundabout just east of the Sussex University buildings at Falmer. Use the bridge crossing immediately south of the mini-roundabout to go over the A27, then take the first right turn and bear right again before the university buildings to arrive at the station.

Section 7 Southease station to Alfriston incorporating trig points at Itford Hill/Firle Beacon **TQ445055/485059.**

Regular trains serving Southease on Brighton-Seaford line; reasonably regular buses serving Alfriston from Berwick(ESCC) and on Berwick-Seaford route(CCB). 7 miles. R Alfriston (P,C,S).

From Southease station, easily reached by train from Falmer, walk briefly eastwards up to the busy A26. Cross this road with care and bear right to just short of a footbridge, here bearing left as signposted and following a clear track which proceeds uphill, soon veering to the right and heading southwards, gaining height all the while. As you climb, look carefully for a left turn - at the time of writing the fingerpost indicating this had broken - and take this left turn, swinging from southwards to north-eastwards and continuing uphill. The path, reasonably well defined, swings eastwards as indicated by another (hopefully intact!) fingerpost and climbs up onto Itford Hill. You pass through a gate and the gradient eases, enabling you to enjoy an easier walk to the Itford Hill trig point which is immediately to the left of the route next to (at the time of writing, bone dry) Red Lion Pond. The views are sensational, particularly to the Ouse valley which you can follow with your eyes all the way from Lewes to the sea. Now having reached the top of the escarpment you can enjoy easy progress north-eastwards then eastwards,

The Itford Hill trig point, superbly set high above the Ouse valley

138

Flying high….a hang-glider high above the trig point on Firle Beacon

passing a radio station and going forward to a car park at the top end of a road which leads down to the village of Firle; from the road crossing you continue in an easterly direction along the top of the escarpment, but are soon confronted by another climb, albeit fairly gentle, and this brings you to the climax of this walk, Firle Beacon. The trig point is immediately adjacent to the route, again to the left. This is a quite magnificent viewpoint and one of the highlights of the SDW as well as your trig point exploration, with glorious views in all directions, including a splendid panorama to the north and north-west. The SDW now swings south-eastwards, maintaining height as it proceeds along Bostal Hill, then drops down steadily and swings eastwards to reach a metalled road and descend to Alfriston (note that much of this walk from Firle Beacon overlaps with the Alfriston-based circular trig point walk number 8 in the East Sussex section of this book). Alfriston is one of the loveliest villages in Sussex and an obvious place to end this section with reasonable bus links and an excellent range of amenities.

Section 8 Alfriston to Eastbourne (coastal route) incorporating trig points
at Haven Brow/Beachy Head **TV525977/591958.**

Reasonably regular buses serving Alfriston from Berwick(ESCC) and on Berwick-Seaford route(CCB); regular trains serving Eastbourne on Brighton-Lewes-Hastings line. 10.5 miles. R Alfriston (P,C,S), Birling Gap (C), Beachy Head (P), Eastbourne (P,C,S).

This walk can be conveniently combined with a march back from Eastbourne to Alfriston via the inland alternative route of the SDW (described in section 9 below) thus creating a giant circular walk, although because of the amount of hill climbing involved you will be pushed to complete it in a day. The walk, starting at Alfriston, begins quietly with a gentle stroll along the left bank of the Cuckmere River southwards to Litlington, where you leave the river. You climb southwards to a good viewpoint above the Cuckmere, then descend to Charleston Manor and enter Friston Forest, emerging from it to enter and pass through the pretty village of Westdean; veering south-westwards, you descend through the forest to cross the A259 close to Exceat and drop down to Cuckmere Haven, the most unspoilt estuary in Sussex. Having arrived at the valley bottom, the SDW quickly bears left, away from the valley-bottom path, shortly rising quite steeply as it proceeds south-eastwards. It soon levels out, but then veers in a more southerly direction and and begins rising again, not too steeply, and comes to a gate; go through the gate and turn immediately left, uphill, to arrive at a trig point on Haven Brow, actually the first of the Seven Sisters cliffs. The views from here to the Cuckmere estuary, Seaford Head and the cliffs are magnificent. From the trig point, descend directly to rejoin the SDW, bearing left to follow it south-eastwards over the Seven Sisters, a tremendous walk. You descend to Birling Gap with its welcome refreshment opportunity, then climb again to pass the Belle Tout lighthouse and, after a brief descent to the road, you ascend to Beachy Head, one of the classic viewpoints on the SDW and indeed on the south coast of Great Britain. The trig point is to the left of the route, on your side of the road, with a popular pub/restaurant just over the road; from the hilltop round the Beachy Head trig point views on a clear day will include Brighton and beyond to the west, and Eastbourne, Pevensey Bay and Bexhill to the east. It's now a long and often quite steep descent north-eastwards to Eastbourne. You arrive at the bottom end of Duke's Drive, going forward to King Edward's Parade and the Eastbourne promenade; now just follow the promenade past the Wish Tower and the RNLI Lifeboat Museum to the junction of Grand Parade with Devonshire Place, turning left into Devonshire Place to access the shopping centre and railway station.

Section 9 Eastbourne to Alfriston (inland route) incorporating trig points on Warren Hill/Willingdon Hill/Wilmington Hill
TV589982/TQ577009/548034.
Public transport as for section 8. 7.5 miles. R Eastbourne(P,C,S), Jevington (P), Alfriston (P,C,S).

To reach the start of the inland route of the SDW, walk back down Grand Parade,

Looking down on Eastbourne from the Willingdon Hill trig point

Eastbourne, from the junction with Devonshire Place (see section 8 immediately above) and shortly - just before the RNLI Lifeboat Museum in fact - turn right into Carlisle Road and follow it just west of south for about a mile to the junction with Gaudick Road and Paradise Drive. Bear half right into Paradise Drive, shortly bearing left to join the SDW and ascend onto Warren Hill, initially just south of west then veering just north of west. You gain height gradually, following a clear green path, and as you do so, look out for the Warren Hill trig point above you to the left; you need to detour briefly up the slope to reach it and enjoy the excellent views to the sea and down to Eastbourne. Return to the route of the SDW and go forward to reach the A259, crossing it with care and now proceeding on an obvious and well-defined track heading just west of north. You gain some more height then descend briefly, passing a pond which is to your right, then climb once more; having reached the top of the rise, you are then faced with another climb, the SDW now veering more decisively north-westwards. At the top of this rise, you reach a crossroads of paths, and you will now see the Willingdon Hill trig point clearly on your right, a short detour away from the SDW and just under 2 miles from the A259 crossing. The views from here on a clear day are superb, with Eastbourne clearly visible below and Pevensey Bay and Bexhill also within sight. From the trig point you return to the SDW, veer in a more westerly direction and drop down to Jevington. Crossing Jevington Road here, you now begin rising again, resuming a more north-westerly direction. In a little under 2 miles from Jevington the ground suddenly falls away dramatically to the left and you'll describe a crude semicircle round the top rim of what is a very steep grassy hillside with a dry valley beneath known as Tenantry Ground. At this point you reach a gate and the SDW swings south-westwards. Pass through the gate and turn immediately right to climb onto the higher ground at Wilmington Hill, keeping the fence to your right and arriving at the Wilmington Hill trig point, the views from which are absolutely magnificent, especially to the South Downs escarpment further west. Return to the SDW and now follow it south-westwards to the fine viewpoint of Windover Hill, veering north-westwards and then just south of west, descending steeply to and crossing a road just above the village of Wilmington. You continue to descend in a north-westerly direction to another road, turning left to follow it just west of south to Plonk Barn, where you bear right to cross the Cuckmere and arrive back in Alfriston.

The Wilmington Hill trig point, high above the Long Man

Long grass guards the trig point at Ringmer (East Sussex, walk 10).

*Monarch of all it surveys - a view of the Highdown Hill
trig point on a cloudless day (West Sussex, walk 27).*